Establishing New Senior Colleges

525

EB RESEARCH MONOGRAPH NUMBER 12 BY A. J. BRUMBAUGH

SOUTHERN REGIONAL EDUCATION BOARD
130 SIXTH STREET, N. W.
ATLANTA, GEORGIA 30313
1966

378.15 B834e

FOREWORD

c./

Today there is a great demand for expanded educational opportunities for the ever-growing number of high school graduates. The responses to this demand are new junior colleges, new senior colleges, and new universities. There is a constant hazard, of course, that some of these institutions may be established at the wrong places for the wrong reasons, or that plans for them will be poorly conceived because important factors are overlooked. This publication is designed to assist in sound planning and development of new senior colleges. The author raises a number of philosophical questions that must be answered by those responsible for locating and designing a new college. He does not discuss these questions in detail, nor does he offer a manual on campus planning and building construction. He does, however, stress the basic considerations that are involved in effective planning and design and that help prevent costly and lasting errors in establishing new senior colleges.

Dr. Brumbaugh, who authored an earlier publication by SREB entitled *Guidelines for the Establishment of Community Junior Colleges*, has had a wide range of experience as a college and university administrator, a consultant to state boards of higher education and to private agencies, a director of state-wide studies of higher education, and as a consultant to or director of planning commissions for new higher institutions. From this experience and from the experience of others he has derived the basic concepts presented here.

The Southern Regional Education Board hopes that this discussion will be helpful to those who are considering the establishment of a new senior college and to those who are in the process of designing one.

WINFRED L. GODWIN, *Director*
Southern Regional Education Board

iii

ACKNOWLEDGMENTS

Many persons have had a part in the preparation of this monograph, some through the channel of publications and source materials; others by direct participation in its production. Credit is given in the monograph to individuals and publications that are the sources of valuable information and points of view. Special credit must be given to colleagues who have been particularly helpful in planning and producing the monograph. Dr. Winfred L. Godwin, Director of SREB, not only approved the project, but gave continuous encouragement while it was in the process of completion. Dr. James L. Miller, Jr. suggested important revisions of the manuscript and put into final form the section on financing new senior colleges. Dr. E. F. Schietinger provided statistical information and organized some of the statistical tables. Mr. William R. O'Connell suggested last minute revisions, made a final check of footnotes and format, and was especially helpful in preparing the manuscript for the editors. Mrs. Gail Crider suggested revisions of the manuscript and provided library resource materials.

Even though many individuals have participated in the preparation and production of the monograph, the author must assume complete responsibility for its content and for the point of view reflected in it.

TABLE OF CONTENTS

LIST OF FIGURES

LIST OF TABLES

CHAPTER 1

INTRODUCTION AND BACKGROUND

An issue of major concern to all educational agencies, public and private, state and Federal, is how to keep post-high school education in step with ever-growing demands. Decisions must be made concerning the kinds of opportunities needed; how they can be made available most economically and effectively — by the expansion of existing institutions, by the establishment of new community colleges, by the establishment of new senior colleges and universities, or by a combination of these provisions.

Several recent publications suggest basic principles and guidelines for the establishment of junior colleges. There are no correspondingly definitive publications regarding the establishment of senior colleges. Both public and private agencies must think clearly and imaginatively in planning new senior colleges adequate to the present and emerging needs of youth and of society. To provide assistance in this planning process is the primary purpose of this brochure.

SCOPE AND TERMINOLOGY

New colleges whose programs lead to the bachelor's degree or, in some instances, to the master's degree are the focus of concern in this discussion. The brochure is not designed to include colleges whose undergraduate programs are professionally oriented, such as architecture, engineering, pharmacy, or business administration, although some of the principles and suggested guidelines may have relevance to such colleges.

The term "senior college" is used throughout the brochure to differentiate the college that grants a bachelor's or master's degree from the junior college on the one hand, and from the undergraduate professional college and the multiple-purpose university

1

on the other hand. It should be noted, however, that the program of a new senior college may cover the span from high school graduation to the baccalaureate or master's degree, or it may be limited to the shorter span from the completion of junior college to the bachelor's or master's degree. Both of these types of institutions come within the purview of this discussion.

SENIOR COLLEGES IN TRANSITION

By and large our senior liberal arts colleges are rooted so deeply in the past that they find it difficult to respond to the demands of a new day. Even so, the liberal arts colleges of today bear little resemblance to their predecessors of a century ago. The changes that they have undergone reflect the impact of various conflicts and pressures. They have experienced conflicts between religious dogma and secular culture, between the concept of education as a liberalizing influence and the concept of education as vocational training, between the efforts to maintain a central unity of liberal education and the rapid segmentation and proliferation of departments and courses, between the pressures for increase in size and commitments to the merits of the small institution, between the increasingly commanding role of publicly supported universities and the need for retaining the distinctive role of the private liberal arts college.

Under the influence of these conflicts and pressures, liberal arts colleges have broadened their purposes, have reduced or abandoned their emphasis on the classics, and have added vocationally oriented programs. In the course of this transition, many liberal arts colleges have lost their focus, become confused, and the fundamentals of liberal education have become submerged in a multiplicity of specializations, both academic and professional.

Even among the colleges that have held to well defined goals while adjusting to the demands of a rapidly changing socioeconomic order are found many differentiating characteristics. Diversity prevails. Each college has distinctive characteristics expressed in its purposes, programs, and services. This is as it should be. Only a monolithic society can justify a monolithic system of higher education.

Because of this diversity there is no model college in the United States. Therefore, each new college must be designed to play its own distinctive role. New ideas and new creative approaches are the key to designing a new senior college for tomorrow.

CONDITIONS THAT LEAD TO THE ESTABLISHMENT OF NEW PUBLIC SENIOR COLLEGES

There has been no systematic inquiry into the reasons for the establishment of new senior colleges. It is possible, however, to identify various combinations of motivating factors by examining the conditions that have led to the recent establishment of some new ones. Because the conditions that justify the establishment of a new private college may be quite different from those giving rise to one that is publicly supported, the reasons for establishment of the two types of institutions are considered separately.

One factor contributing to the origin of new state colleges is the growing recognition that education beyond the high school is both desirable and essential. It is desirable because to be well educated is a source of personal satisfaction and is a badge of social distinction. Going to college has become the vogue. It is essential because of the rising educational requirements for employment and because of the increasing complexity of political, economic, and social problems on which citizens must make sound decisions. Not only have these factors contributed to the constantly rising level of education of our citizens, but also they have made the public more and more favorably disposed to providing appropriate post-high school opportunities for all who can profit from them. Some states have explicitly stated this as public policy; others have expressed it by implication. The demand for more education for more individuals gives rise to the need for new colleges.

A second factor is the establishment of barriers against out-of-state students. As the pressures on state colleges and universities increase so that they find it difficult to accommodate out-of-state students, admission requirements and out-of-state tuition are raised. In fact, according to recent reports, some state universities and land-grant colleges set non-resident undergraduate tuition and fees at more than three times the amount charged resident students. For example, the charges in 1965 for non-residents and residents in a few states where the differences are large are: Arizona $880 - $230; California $1020 - $220; University of Colorado $1120 - $372; University of Wisconsin $1050 - $320. While the differential in other states is not as great as in those cited, it is generally large enough to constitute a substantial barrier to non-residents. Along with high fees and higher scholastic requirements for out-of-state students, limitations are also placed on dormitory and other accommodations for non-residents. The effect of this policy on debtor states — those that have more out-migration than in-migration of students — is to further increase the demand for post-high school educational opportunities within the parent states. The possible impact of such a change in policy can be judged by the following table and map showing the facts on in- and out-of-state migration.

Table 1—Enrollment and Migration of All College Students, All Institutions, United States and SREB States, Fall 1963

State	Students Enrolled	Migration of Students		
		Out of	Into	Net
United States..........	4,233,501	775,198	849,624	+74,426
SREB States............	1,042,989	176,060	195,742	+19,682
Alabama................	45,261	9,281	8,559	— 722
Arkansas...............	31,311	5,632	4,445	— 1,187
Florida.................	100,646	22,047	13,435	— 8,612
Georgia................	55,744	11,941	12,941	+ 1,000
Kentucky...............	55,873	9,436	14,136	+ 4,700
Louisiana..............	69,090	6,166	9,100	+ 2,934
Maryland...............	63,589	22,882	13,265	— 9,617
Mississippi.............	40,940	5,061	6,525	+ 1,464
North Carolina..........	83,202	9,129	23,716	+14,587
Oklahoma..............	65,407	7,029	10,697	+ 3,668
South Carolina.........	33,811	7,749	9,943	+ 2,194
Tennessee..............	73,708	11,193	22,128	+10,935
Texas..................	228,090	16,755	22,296	+ 5,541
Virginia................	62,321	26,439	16,239	—10,200
West Virginia..........	33,996	5,320	8,317	+ 2,997

Source: U.S. Office of Education, *Residence and Migration of College Students, Fall 1963 State and Regional Data*, U.S. Government Printing Office, Washington, 1965, adapted from Table 1, p. 29.

A third important condition leading to the establishing of new state colleges is the distance of many state higher institutions from growing centers of population. Until the last decade or two, the locations of state universities and colleges were determined largely by political and economic considerations. There were no state-wide plans. Often there were no large centers of population. In recent decades population has become more and more concentrated in metropolitan areas. More than 84 percent of the American people now live in 212 metropolitan areas, and these same areas encompass 80 percent of our productive industry. Even though many of our state colleges and universities are located apart from

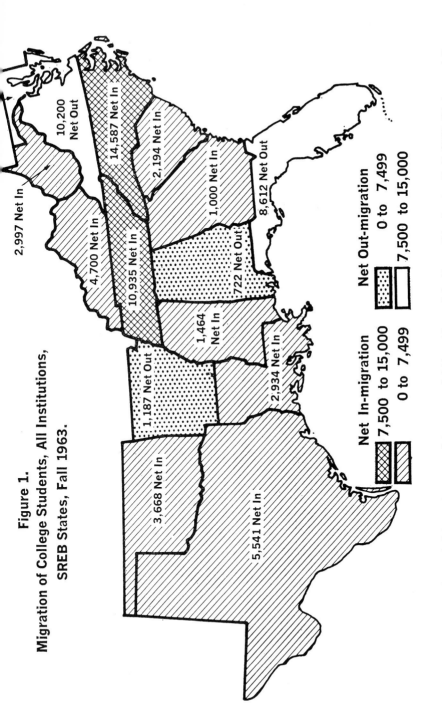

**Figure 1.
Migration of College Students, All Institutions,
SREB States, Fall 1963.**

2,997 Net In

10,200 Net Out

14,587 Net In

2,194 Net In

1,000 Net In

8,612 Net Out

4,700 Net In

10,935 Net In

722 Net Out

1,464 Net In

1,187 Net Out

2,934 Net In

3,668 Net In

5,541 Net In

Net In-migration
7,500 to 15,000
0 to 7,499

Net Out-migration
0 to 7,499
7,500 to 15,000

Source: U.S. Office of Education. *Residence and Migration of College Students, Fall 1963 State and Regional Data,* U.S. Government Printing Office, 1965. Figure 1, p. 10.

5

these growing metropolitan areas, generally they have all the students they can accommodate. There still remain large numbers of students in the metropolitan areas for whom provisions must be made.

Fourth, political factors and local community interests still influence, sometimes unduly, the establishment of new colleges. Nor is it any wonder that communities and cities compete with one another for a new college or university, for it is both a cultural and an economic asset. It is big business. It is not surprising, therefore, that members of legislatures lobby for a new college in their districts and that governors make campaign promises of new colleges in return for political support. Strong as these forces may be in promoting the establishment of new colleges, they do not provide a sound basis for deciding what type of college, if any, is needed or where it should be located.

A fifth factor is the necessity of setting some kind of limit on the size of existing institutions. There are no objectively established maximum enrollments for colleges or universities. It is recognized, however, that more and more of the state-supported higher institutions are becoming so large that their effectiveness tends to be impaired. When limits on enrollments in existing institutions are set, as they have been in California and as they are proposed in several other states, the demand for new institutions is intensified.

CONDITIONS THAT LEAD TO THE ESTABLISHMENT OF NEW PRIVATE SENIOR COLLEGES

Whenever a question of establishing a new private senior college arises, one of the first questions that should be asked is, "Why?" "On what grounds can such a step be justified?"

First, it should be noted that individuals and agencies that promote and support new private colleges are responsive to the growing demands for post-high school educational opportunities. In this respect they are dedicated to the public interest. But in responding to this demand, they are also motivated by the need for certain religious and ethical emphases which it is believed are missing in public higher education.

This point of view is expressed clearly and succinctly in a *Report on the Establishment of a New Private Church-Related College,* as follows:

> The Christian college is an integral part of the church's educational program and the most appropriate place for the maturing of religious concepts started in church and home. The college

6

enrolls youth in a very impressionable period of their development. It is most important, therefore, for it to surround them with an atmosphere which will be conducive to the forming of a Christian philosophy of life. Students in the church college acquire as a part of their educational experience a knowledge and a real understanding of the Christian faith.[1]

The leaders in the area of private higher education are moved, therefore, to establish new colleges that will give society leaders firmly grounded in ethics and religion.

A second motivating factor is to preserve and strengthen denominational identity. This is especially true among religious groups that are dedicated to the perpetuation of particular dogma and ceremonial practices. Most impressive in this regard has been the growth in the number of Catholic colleges in the United States — from 253 in 1954 to 366 in 1965 — an increase of approximately 50 percent in a decade. Also strongly committed to denominational purposes are those maintained and controlled by the Lutheran, Seventh-Day Adventist, Baptist, and other protestant groups.

Most protestant church-related colleges do not stress a denominational emphasis. They place their emphasis on religious commitment. More and more the church-related colleges are moving to a liberal view that stresses scholarship and learning linked with commitment to the ethical and religious values inherent in the Judaeo-Christian tradition. But, the more conservative the group supporting or controlling the college, the greater is the likelihood that the faculty will be required to make a declaration of theological beliefs and that students will be indoctrinated in the beliefs held by the church.

A third reason for the establishment of a new private college is to fill a gap in the educational resources of an area or to establish a balance among various types of higher institutions in the area. *A Study of Potentials for a Christian College in Hawaii,* made a few years ago, stated that a new church-related college would

> ... help the new state to retain many potential leaders needed for its future development who now remain on the mainland after they graduate from mainland colleges. It will cultivate and strengthen the Christian qualities of character and service that are basic to the effective operation of a democratic society. It will become a major factor in the cultural enrichment of the islands.[2]

---

[1]*Report on the Establishment of a Presbyterian College in Florida.* For information about this report address inquiries to the President, Florida Presbyterian College, St. Petersburg, Florida.

[2]A. J. Brumbaugh, *A Study of the Potentials for the Christian College in Hawaii* (Nashville, Tennessee: Division of Higher Education, Methodist Board of Education).

A fourth reason underlying the establishment of a new private college is to demonstrate the validity of an educational philosophy or a point of view.

Other factors are: to fulfill the wishes of a philanthropist, to honor a distinguished religious or educational leader, or to capitalize on the momentum and resources generated by a local community. Usually there is more than one reason for founding a new private senior college. Contributory factors will occur in various combinations, but one or two among those noted are generally of primary importance.

CHAPTER 2

PLANNING AND ESTABLISHING
A NEW COLLEGE

THE IMPORTANCE OF A MASTER PLAN

Both efficiency and effectiveness in higher education demand that each new post-high school institution, be it a junior college, senior college, professional school, or university, fit into a comprehensive plan for all higher institutions in the state or region. Our national landscape is dotted with the sites of colleges that have passed into oblivion — almost two-thirds of some 500 established during the middle of the last century. In many instances, not even a cornerstone remains to mark the spot. The demise of some of these institutions may not have been a real loss to higher education, but their rise and fall, in many instances, was a wasteful experience. In responding to the demands of our day we cannot afford to spend our human and economic resources on misconceived and misplaced institutions. Yet examples could be cited even now of new institutions that perpetuate historical errors.

To avoid the errors of the past, each state, in the case of publicly supported institutions, must formulate a plan that delineates the role and scope of each existing college or university; that indicates the types of additional institutions that are needed and the geographical area in which they should be located. This kind of planning is no less important for a church board or other private agency than for a state board. The church or agency should have an overall design of the number and kinds of institutions it needs and can support and where they should be located.

Planning should begin with a clearly formulated statement of guiding principles — an educational creed. This we believe! The statement may be focused on the needs of individuals who are destined to become leaders, on the needs of all participants in our democracy, or on the needs of society itself to keep it in step with

9

technological and economic changes. In fact, both individual and societal needs should be arrived at by careful analytical thinking on the part of those who are responsible for planning.

But the formulation of a statement of guiding principles is only the first of several important steps that must be taken in the preparation of a master plan. Other steps are:

— to formulate an overview of need for education beyond the high school;

— to appraise present post-high school educational opportunities and resources, public and private;

— to project opportunities needed beyond those currently or potentially available;

— to define the role and scope of present higher institutions, public and private;

— to evolve from these studies and appraisals a master plan for higher education.

These steps are so interrelated that they should not be undertaken on a piecemeal basis. The whole concept of master planning requires that competent, professional personnel be responsible for outlining, directing or conducting, and coordinating each of these steps. Such comprehensive and systematic approaches to master planning are most commonly found in connection with state-supported higher education. For purposes of illustration, a few typical procedures are noted.

The Board of Control for Higher Education in Florida (now designated the Board of Regents) started the development of a master plan by appointing a Council for the Study of Higher Education — a group of five specialists in higher education from outside the state. The Council nominated one of its own members to serve as director of the study. The director, with the assistance of a small professional staff, prepared an outline of the study which, when approved by the Council and the Board of Control, defined the premises and scope of the study. The study included all higher institutions, public and private. With the assistance of a number of specialists in such fields as demography, economics, professional programs, graduate education, student personnel services, extension education, educational costs, business management of institutions, and operations of the Board of Control, a report was prepared consisting of a summary volume and four volumes of supporting data and special studies.

10

The recommendations made by the Council constituted the starting point for the development of a system of community colleges and for the establishment of new, degree-granting institutions. These developments had not proceeded far before the need for a second stage in planning became apparent, namely, the delineation of the role of each publicly supported senior institution in the university system and the scope of its offerings. In response to this need, the executive officer of the Board of Control appointed an interinstitutional committee to plan a "role and scope" study. A comprehensive outline was prepared by the committee with the advice of an outside consultant who had been the director of the Council's study. Each senior institution was asked to make a comprehensive self-study with a view to defining its own role in the university system and the scope of its programs considered essential to the achievement of its objectives.

The institutional reports, some of which comprise several good-sized volumes were analyzed and consolidated in the office of the Executive Director of the Board of Control for the purpose of identifying interinstituitonal duplications and gaps in proposed institutional programs. Where serious conflicts or duplications in programs appeared, outside consultants, agreed upon by the Executive Director of the Board and the presidents of the universities concerned, were invited to study the situation and to make recommendations for the resolution of the conflicts.

The final step in this series of developments was the preparation of a master plan for public post-high school education by the staff of the Board of Control — a plan that was officially approved by the Board.

The State of Oklahoma affords another illustration of a centralized responsibility for state-wide planning of higher education. The Constitution of the State provides that the State Regents for Higher Education, a board of nine members, shall be the coordinating agency for the state higher educational system. Among the duties of the Regents is the "compilation and analysis of information about higher education which is essential to state-wide planning and coordination."

At the request of the state legislature and with funds appropriated for the purpose, the Regents authorized in 1961 a study of higher education in the state. For this purpose the Chancellor of the University System augmented his staff by the appointment of a coordinator of research, whose primary responsibility was to plan and conduct the state-wide study. Unlike the Florida study which was planned and conducted by a council of specialists from outside the state, the Oklahoma study was planned and conducted by the staff of the Regents with the assistance of advisory committees and outside consultants. To give assurance that this would be truly a state-wide "self-study," a primary advisory committee to the research staff was made up of the presidents of the 18 institutions in the state system and five presidents of independent and municipal colleges and universities in the state.

The plan for conducting the study also provided that the coordinator of research appoint *ad hoc* problem area advisory committees to help identify available resources of data, develop questionnaires and report forms, and evaluate preliminary findings.

The general purposes of this study were:

1. to identify the needs of the people of the state for education beyond the high school;

2. to make an inventory and analysis of resources — programs, staffs, finances, and facilities — now available for meeting the needs of higher education;

3. to determine ways in which present resources and possible additional resources that may be required may be best used to achieve objectives of higher education in Oklahoma;

4. to inform the governor, the legislature, and citizens of the state about the problems and needs of Oklahoma higher education and about recommendations for improving its quality and effectiveness.

The major problem areas included in the study were:

1. functions and goals of Oklahoma higher education;

2. control and administration;

3. higher education enrollments and projections;

4. higher education opportunities and needs;

5. selecting, retaining, and utilizing faculties and administrative personnel;

6. physical facilities for higher education;

7. financing current operating costs of higher education.

The plan for conducting this study required its extension over a longer time span than is usually involved when such a study is made by a council as in Florida, or by a special commission as in a number of other states. It has the advantage of being truly a state-wide self-study. The deep involvement of all the institutions of the state makes for a more ready acceptance of the findings and recommendations.

As the study nears completion the Regents are facing the most crucial issue, namely, the formulation of a master plan that will on the one hand define the role and scope of each existing institution, and on the other hand designate the number and kind of additional institutions that are needed and where they should be located. This is the heart of state-wide planning.

Still another approach to state-wide study and planning of higher education was made by the Higher Education Study Commission of Virginia.[1] The Commission appointed by the Governor in accordance with legislative authorization consisted of twenty-one members. The Commission appointed a staff to make the study and approved an outline of the topics to be covered. The scope of the study is indicated by the subjects of staff reports which are:

Prospective College-age Population in Virginia, by Subregions 1960-1985.

State-wide Pattern of Higher Education in Virginia.

Geographical Origins of Students Attending College in Virginia.

The Two-year College in Virginia.

Instructional Programs in Virginia's Institutions of Higher Education.

Educational Programs in Virginia for Fields Related to Health.

Extension Services, Television Instruction, and Research in Virginia's Institutions of Higher Education.

The Faculties of Virginia's Colleges and Universities.

Library Services in Virginia's Institutions of Higher Education.

Instructional Plants in Virginia's Institutions of Higher Education.

Control and Coordination of Higher Education in Virginia.

The 1965 Report of the Commission presents recommendations, some of which require legislative action, others, action by

[1] Higher Education Study Commission Report, 11 Volumes. Richmond, Virginia, 1965.

13

the State Council for Higher Education, still others, action by the boards or administrators and faculties of the institutions.

This approach to state-wide study and planning is distinctive because it was completed in a shorter time than such studies usually require and because the responsibility for conducting the study was concentrated in a single highly competent and respected expert from outside the state.

There are other approaches to master planning than those followed in Florida, Oklahoma, and Virginia. The legislatures of other states have also authorized or promulgated the appointment of special commissions to study educational needs and to propose plans for the coordination and orderly development of needed educational facilities. In some states, e.g., California, Illinois, Maryland, and Utah, the recommendations of such commissions have led to the establishment of a permanent coordinating body.

The purpose of this discussion is not to consider in detail either the functions or the merits of these various approaches to planning, but to stress the point that any new publicly supported senior college should be conceived and authorized as an essential unit in a state-wide plan. This approach can safeguard quality; it can prevent unnecessary rivalry and duplication; it can delineate the differentiating characteristics of institutions; it can define priorities in the needs for new institutions; and it can enlist the support of an informed constituency. Before considering further specific factors that must be taken into account in the establishment of a new senior college, it is important to note in what respects master planning of private colleges differs from planning those that are publicly supported.

Private colleges fall into two broad categories — those that are closely related to a religious body and those that are largely or completely independent of such an affiliation. There are variations in the degree to which church-related colleges are controlled and supported by the denomination to which they are related.

A number of denominations have a central administrative unit that is specifically and in many cases exclusively responsible for the higher education interests of the church. In some respects these boards correspond to coordinating bodies and boards established by state governments.

Data presented in a report on *Church-Related Boards Responsible for Higher Education*[2] show a wide variation among these

---

[2]James C. Messersmith, *Church-Related Boards Responsible for Higher Education*, U.S. Office of Education Bulletin No. 1964, No. 13 (Washington, D. C.: U.S. Government Printing Office, 1964).

boards as to the degree of control they exercise over colleges of their respective denomination.

Some boards exercise a considerable degree of authority by establishing regulations governing institutional affiliation with a board and by setting conditions prerequisite to participating in denominational financial support. For example, the University Senate of the Methodist Church has formulated criteria for giving institutions recognition and for eligibility to participate in support provided by the Division of Higher Education. The Senate may investigate institutions as to objectives, programs, standards, personnel, plant and equipment, student personnel services, public relations, religious life or other aspects. Also, no institution that is designed to have an affiliation with the Methodist Senate and the Methodist Division of Higher Education can be established or acquired without prior approval of the Senate and the Division of Higher Education. Thus, the initiative for establishing a new college is taken by a local conference or local conferences, but the approval or disapproval of such action is given by the central agency. The coordination and control of Methodist Colleges, old and new, is achieved by recognition of colleges that comply with specified standards both for prestige and for financial support.

A comparatively high degree of control over its higher institutions is indicated by the functions of the Board of Higher Education, The Lutheran Church, Missouri Synod. While this Board is not endowed with governing powers giving it direct control of institutional operations, it does, in fact, exercise a fairly high degree of control through its coordinating functions. It is in an extraordinarily powerful position because all salaries of instructional personnel and most capital funds are paid by the Synodical Treasury. In total, about half of the operating funds of the colleges are subsidized by the church. This direct participation in financing the colleges leads to the assumption of major responsibility by the Board of Higher Education and ultimately by the Board of Directors of the Church in such matters as approval of educational programs, review of budgets, approval of permanent tenure for staff members, acquisition of sites for new colleges, purchase of land for existing colleges and planning and financing of new buildings.

While national church boards of higher education exert varying degrees of direction and control over colleges under their aegis, it appears from all the data available that none of these boards has engaged in comprehensive studies and planning with a view to determining the need for new colleges, the type of colleges needed and their location.

15

Several boards, like the Education Commission of the Southern Baptist Convention, have promoted an interest on the part of state conventions, synods, or conferences in studying the needs for new institutions. The Commission, at the request of state conventions, made a study of the potentials for Baptist colleges in certain metropolitan areas. But both the initiative and the final decision regarding the establishment of new colleges rested with the State Conventions.

The General Conference of the Seventh-Day Adventist Church apparently exercises more than the usual amount of leadership in controlling and planning the establishment of new colleges or changing the status of existing ones, as is indicated by the following statement of policy:

1. General Conference approval shall be required in the locating and establishing of junior and senior colleges or the equivalents, the raising of a secondary school to advanced status, the raising of a junior college to senior college status, and the establishment of graduate and postgraduate programs in all the divisions of the world field.

2. Such authorization shall be sought directly from the General Conference by unions of the North American Division, and, in the case of overseas unions, from the General Conference by and through the division concerned.

3. The request for authorization to establish an advanced school or to elevate an existing school to more advanced status shall be accompanied by a report from an inspection committee appointed by the division or union conference in which the school is located or proposed; this report to describe the purposes of the institution and the field it is to serve, the plans for financing and staffing it, and, in the case of an established school, the proposed change of organization and scholastic level. In the North American Division a representative from the General Conference Department shall be a member of the inspection committee; in the overseas divisions the secretary of education of the division shall be a member of the inspection committee, and whenever possible a representative of the General Conference Department of Education.

4. Plans to establish a new advanced school or to raise a secondary school to advanced level, or to raise a junior college to senior college status shall not be implemented or publicized before General Conference approval has been received.

Regarding the founding of new church-related colleges Wicke says, "In nearly all churches — both protestant and Catholic — the locus of decision is usually regional or local, and local groups are thinking in terms of local needs and ambitions. Church bodies in national sessions may establish principles and guide-

16

lines; it is the local governing bodies that to a large degree determine what is to be done."[3] Among the independent colleges, some still have the marks of a one-time church affiliation while others are and always have been completely free from any such connection.

A brief resumé of how a few new private colleges — church-related and independent — came into being will illustrate the complex of factors involved.

College A is a church-related liberal arts college. Several church leaders in the state proposed the establishment of a church-related college. In response to their suggestion, the church synod authorized the appointment of a council of forty-one church leaders and officers in the state to study the opportunities and responsibilities for the establishment of a college. The council engaged two distinguished educators, who were familiar with study techniques, to serve as co-directors of the study. With the aid of several nationally recognized consultants, a well documented report was prepared which contained the recommendation that a "good liberal arts college under_____auspices should be established in _____." The report contained a summary of a number of important conditions that should be taken into account later in establishing the college.

College B is a protestant college. The establishment of this college resulted from an unusual combination of circumstances. Leaders in the protestant churches of the state, suggested the need for a new protestant college. The question was considered by a church board of higher education to which it was initially directed. A quick preliminary survey tentatively confirmed the need for such a college. The next step was to enlist the cooperation of a second church board which had extensive religious interests in the state. Under the joint auspices of the two boards, a more comprehensive study was made by an educator, experienced in making such studies, with the aid of a number of consultants, of the potentials for a Christian college. The report concluded that "there is need for a residential, coeducational, inter-denominational Christian college of high quality." The report also stated conditions that should be met before plans for the establishment of the college were put into effect. These conditions have been substantially fulfilled and the college is now on the way to becoming a reality.

Colleges C and D are liberal arts colleges related to the same church organization. These two institutions were established simul-

---

[3]Myron F. Wicke, *The Church-Related College*, (New York: The Center for Applied Research in Education, 1964), pp. 7-8.

taneously in the same state under the auspices of the state conference of the supporting denomination. All available information seems to indicate that the two colleges were the outgrowth of competition. Each of two communities sought to attract a college of another denomination which was to be located somewhere within the state. Both were disappointed. Because of the interest that had been aroused and the substantial financial underwriting that had been secured in each community, an appeal was made to the presiding bishop of a different denomination of the area for authorization to establish a college under church auspices. With the concurrence and leadership of the bishop and with the official endorsement of the state conference, the two colleges were authorized. One of the deciding factors apparently was the large financial support each community offered as an inducement. Apparently there were no comprehensive studies, other than those made by the communities themselves, preliminary to the action authorizing the establishment of these two institutions.

These three cases illustrate different approaches to planning a new private senior college: one, a comprehensive study under the auspices of a state church synod; another, a study conducted for two cooperating national church boards; the third, action taken by a state church conference in response to inducements offered by two competing communities.

To these should be added illustrations of planning or the lack thereof in the establishment of new independent senior colleges. The establishment of this type of institution is generally the outcome of local initiative.

More often than not, initiative for establishing a new independent private college is taken by forward-looking and enterprising citizens whose enthusiasm stems quite as much from the benefits the community will derive from such a development as from the educational needs the institution will serve. Too often no comprehensive study is made to justify the establishment of an independent college. In the words of one president, "The fact that every national survey indicates a shortage of school space was enough to convince us that we could obtain the number of students we needed . . . . While this may not sound too professional, I would not have been too swayed one way or the other by any local studies as to need because we were only counting on (the state) to furnish between 30-40% of our student body — and this is just about the ratio of our charter class."

In the same vein another president observed, "No study or survey was necessarily made to demonstrate the need of a college. We knew from the statistics available that a college would succeed."

18

There are instances, of course, of more objective justifications. The following cases will suffice to illustrate how independent private colleges come into being.

Hampshire College. This college is still in the planning stage. It is a cooperative enterprise of three private colleges — Amherst, Mount Holyoke, Smith — and the University of Massachusetts. In 1958 a proposal entitled A New College Plan and characterized as a "major departure in higher education" was presented to the presidents of the sponsoring institutions by a special committee. Since then the plan has been under discussion and currently is being reviewed and revised. The college, when it becomes operative, will be unique in its origin and distinctive in its program. It is being designed to "provide education of the highest quality at a minimum cost per student."

An unusual feature of this development is that several established higher institutions, three private and one public, have together conceived and founded the new college. Several distinctive characteristics of the program are: rigid departmental lines will be done away with; a limited number of courses will be offered; a staff of fifty instructors will be adequate for a student body of 1000; students will be encouraged to take advanced courses at any of the cooperating institutions; as they advance in the program students will be guided toward independent work; for one month each academic year the whole student body will participate in two courses, one in some aspect of western and one in some aspect of non-western culture.

The College of Oak Ridge. This college, chartered in 1964, is expected to become operative in the Fall of 1967. It is a community enterprise promoted by leading citizens. While the arguments advanced in support of the project are largely subjective, they do suggest that more critical thinking has gone into the development of plans than is characteristic of some new institutional plans.

Some of the advantages attributed to the location and to the establishment of the college are: Oak Ridge is a highly science-oriented community in which there are good facilities for teaching the sciences in a liberal arts college. The college would bring to a scientific community a "fuller appreciation of the humanities and the social sciences; the college will provide educational opportunities to a large number of high school graduates in East Tennessee who have the potential to succeed in college, but do not attend college." Again, it may be said that these justifications are largely subjective, but they are supported to a degree by objective data.

Changing the Status of Junior Colleges. This discussion would be incomplete if it did not include consideration of the extension of junior colleges to senior college status. These are not new colleges in the strict sense of the term, but they are new as senior colleges. The magnitude of this development is indicated by the fact that from 1953-54 to 1963-64, 72 junior colleges changed to senior college status. Of these, only 11 had enrollments of 1,000 or more. As to type of control, 11 were public; 23 were independent; and 38 church-related.

Of major concern are, or should be, the motivating forces that bring about this upward extension of junior colleges. How do they fit into developmental plans? What are the losses as well as the gains?

The reasons for the changes from junior to senior college status have not been studied systematically. Among the arguments that have been advanced by proponents of such changes are the following:

1. The junior college is in a period of transition from identification with the public school system to an independent status in the arena of higher education. Complete identification with higher education is to be achieved by becoming a senior college.

2. More and more faculty members in junior colleges are recruited from senior colleges and the graduate schools of universities. They are less completely oriented to and committed to the distinctive role of the junior college than are those who have been identified with the public schools. Therefore, they support, sometimes even promote, the conversion of a junior college into a senior institution.

3. Private junior colleges may feel the impingement of public junior colleges that are established in close geographical proximity and be impelled in self-defense to move to senior college status.

4. Political influences within legislative circles sometimes promote the upward extension of junior colleges for the purpose of transferring major sources of support from the local community to the state, thereby increasing public benefit to their constituents.

5. A legislator frequently feels that a senior college in his district elevates the status of the community and adds to his own prestige.

Generally, the change over of a junior college into a senior college represents a loss as well as a gain. Too often the loss is greater than the gain. The loss arises from the neglect or exclusion of certain educational functions by senior colleges that are basic to the services of comprehensive junior colleges. For example, comprehensive junior colleges offer college parallel programs that enable students to continue more advanced study in the senior university comparable to programs provided in the freshman and sophomore years of senior colleges; but beyond this the comprehensive junior college provides a coherent program of terminal general or technical-vocational education for students who, for any reason, are unable to continue their education beyond the junior college. The junior college also offers programs of continuing education to assist adults to meet changing educational, economic, and cultural conditions. When a junior college is given senior college status, its perspective becomes narrower and its emphasis tends to be placed on the academic program to the neglect of broader types of educational services, which are regarded as incompatible with the purposes of a senior college. In the words of the *Regents Tentative State-wide Plan for the Expansion and Development of Higher Education* in the State of New York, "Two-year and four-year colleges in a planned, coordinated, and complete system of public higher education provide essential and complementary but distinctive services in post-high school education. Therefore, existing two-year colleges should not be converted to four-year baccalaureate college status as an approach to the expansion of college programs in any region in the state."

Either as a matter of policy or of legislative action, steps are taken in some states to preserve the status of the community junior college by providing, on the one hand, that it shall not be authorized to become a senior college; and on the other hand, that no public senior college shall be established in an area prior to the establishment of a public junior college. These provisions suggest that where the need for a senior college is demonstrated, it should be established *de novo*.

These considerations point to the need for a new type of upper division institution which begins at the junior year and provides programs of two or three years leading to the bachelor's or master's degree. Several institutions of this type are already in operation and still others are being contemplated. They rely on junior colleges to provide the first two years of undergraduate education and, by means of testing and counseling services, to identify those students who have the qualifications and the preparation to continue

21

their studies beyond the junior college.

Several conclusions may be drawn from the preceding illustrations and discussions concerning planning of new senior colleges.

First, a growing number of states have formulated long-range plans for the development of a coordinated system of public higher education. These plans are usually derived from a comprehensive study of the population growth, economic trends, manpower needs, present and potential capacities of existing institutions, expenditures, financial resources, and other factors that have a bearing on the need for a new college. The plans generally include a consideration of the need for new post-high school institutions of various types, their location, priorities for their establishment, and estimated costs as a guide to legislatures in making necessary appropriations.

Second, a number of states have not yet reached the stage of comprehensive planning. In these states new colleges of whatever type are generally established in response to population pressures often combined with political considerations.

Third, there has been too little comprehensive, systematic planning for private senior colleges. Church boards or similar agencies generally rely on state conferences or synods or local communities to initiate plans for a new college. Only occasionally has a central church board taken the lead in exploring the need for new colleges.

It appears, furthermore, that too often new private colleges are founded on opportunistic inducements rather than objective evidence of need. Even so, if well administered and financed, these colleges may make a significant contribution to the cause of higher education.

Up to this point consideration has been centered on broad background issues related to the establishment of a new senior college — the changing character of the liberal arts college; conditions that lead to the establishment of new senior colleges; and the importance of an overall plan for the development of higher education under public or private auspices.

Certain crucial questions affecting the establishment of a new senior college remain to be considered, e.g., What are the indices of need for a new senior college? What kind of college is needed? Where should it be located? What personnel, professional and non-professional, will be required to staff the college? What are the specific requirements for an appropriate site? What are the successive steps in planning physical facilities? What important factors are to be kept in mind in planning physical facilities? What considerations enter into estimating cost for capital outlay for operation? What plans for financing a new senior college have proven most satisfactory? What special problems and pitfalls should be anticipated? These questions will be discussed in terms of guiding principles derived from specific cases, some of which will be cited. Reference will be made to some of the manuals and source materials that provide more precise and detailed information on some of these issues.

THE DETERMINATION OF NEED FOR A NEW SENIOR COLLEGE

The importance of a comprehensive plan for new colleges has just been stressed. Central to the formulation of a comprehensive plan is the determination of need. There are no clearly defined criteria of need for a new senior college — public or private. Furthermore, the procedures and factors considered in the establishment of a new publicly supported senior college differ from those leading to the establishment of a privately supported college. Therefore, the determination of need for the establishment of each of the two types of colleges will be considered separately.

With reference to the public senior colleges it should be noted first that most of the comprehensive state-wide plans for higher education include provisions for a system or network of junior colleges or branches of state universities to make post-high school opportunities widely available; for senior colleges to afford opportunities for education of the baccalaureate or master's degree level and for an educational capstone of a state university or a university system. The needs for a new state college are, therefore, interwoven with indices of need for other types of post-high school institutions. An examination of how the needs for certain new state colleges were determined suggests the most important factors that were taken into account.

The most effective procedure already noted under statewide planning, judged both by its widespread use and by practical results, is an overall appraisal of the state's future educational needs and of the potential of existing institutions to meet these needs. Specifically, such an appraisal will include projected college enrollments by five-year intervals; projected professional and technical manpower needs indicated by the evolving economy; estimates of the maximum capacity of existing institutions for efficient operation; the number of potential students for whom additional opportunities must be provided at specified dates; the efficacy of existing programs to meet future needs; and the location of presently operating institutions in relation to growing centers of population.

A brief review of the experiences of several states in deciding on the need for new senior colleges will indicate which of these factors were considered and how they were interpreted. The Council for the Study of Higher Education in Florida, in its report made in 1956, projected a threefold increase in college enrollments from 44,500 to 132,000 in 1970. A later projection indicated that the 1970 enrollment would be at least 158,000 and probably even higher. As a basis for relating higher education to the developing economy of the state, a number of widely recognized economists analyzed the Florida economy and projected the direction and potentials of its growth. From the Council's study were derived forecasts of professional manpower needs. Two conclusions arrived at were: that professional training would have to be greatly expanded to meet growing manpower requirements, and that the state was faced with an urgent need for the technical-vocational and semi-professional programs at less than baccalaureate degree level. The former is a function of a degree granting institution; the latter falls in the sphere of the community junior college.

The Council for the Study of Higher Education in Florida pointed out in its report that:

> While there is a diversity of institutions concentrated in northern and central Florida, facilities for education beyond the high school are not uniformly available throughout the state and large population centers are without ready access to public institutions of higher learning. Existing state universities by 1960, will have reached such a size that they will not require additional undergraduate enrollments to enable them to provide undergraduate instruction on an economical basis; but the addition of substantial residential space, as well as some special purpose nonresidential space, will be required to enable these institutions to make full use of present facilities.

> Unless provision is made for enrollment for larger numbers of students in expanded or new private institutions, in community colleges, and in new state degree-granting institutions, it may be necessary to enlarge the existing state universities as much as four or fivefold.[4]

The Council observed that the alternatives to the expansion of existing institutions beyond manageable size were to establish new institutions or to limit admissions, thereby depriving worthy students of the advantage of post-high school education.

---

[4]A. J. Brumbaugh and Myron R. Blee, *Higher Education and Florida's Future* (Gainesville, Florida: University of Florida Press, 1956) p. xvi.

Following the Council's recommendation, there was established a system of junior colleges which enrolled approximately 46,000 students in 1964. The original prediction was an enrollment of 41,000 by 1970. It was further recommended that new degree-granting institutions be established in the Tampa Bay area and on the lower east coast. The reasons were: (1) The existing universities by 1960 would have reached an enrollment large enough to assure economical operation of instructional programs and efficient utilization of facilities. Said the report, "Once an institution has obtained such size that it can operate a broad range of programs on an economical basis, the relief of pressure for expansion frees the staff for concentration on upgrading the quality of services rendered." (2) The sections of the state identified for new state degree-granting institutions had large and growing concentrations of population quite far removed from any of the existing state universities. (3) It was predicted that enrollment in each of the two proposed new institutions would be 10,000 by 1970. Subsequent developments have indicated that these enrollment estimates were too low.

Further studies of potential post-high school enrollments and of economic developments in Florida have resulted in approval of two additional degree-granting institutions — one on the central east coast and one in the extreme western part of the state.

The Council's concept of these new institutions was that they should be degree-granting colleges intermediate between junior colleges and the universities. So rapid has been the growth of the college-age population and so great is the demand for professional manpower that the original concept of the state college has already been abandoned and the new degree-granting institutions have been given university status. This does not invalidate the procedures employed to determine need; instead, it highlights the necessity for continuously reviewing and updating any state-wide plan.

The Master Plan for Higher Education in California reviews and updates data derived from a restudy of the needs of California in higher education and presents recommendations for the establishment of additional state colleges. Several principles of organization of state-supported higher education in California should be noted.

1. The state system of higher education consists of junior colleges, the state colleges, and the University of California which has several campuses. Junior colleges are locally administered, but are coordinated by the State Board of Education; state colleges are administered by

the Trustees of the State College System of California; the university is under the control of a Board of Regents. These three segments of higher education are coordinated by an advisory body, the Coordinating Council for Higher Education.

2. The Coordinating Council for Higher Education is responsible, among other things, for the "development of plans for the orderly growth of higher education and making of recommendations to the governing boards on the need for and location of new facilities and programs."[5]

3. By action of the governing boards "No new state colleges or campuses of the University, other than those already approved, shall be established until adequate junior college facilities have been provided, the determination of adequacy to be based on studies made under the direction of the Liaison Committee* of the State Board of Education and the Regents of the University of California . . . with the further provision that new state colleges and campuses of the University established by action of the Legislature of 1957 and by action of the Regents, also in 1957, be limited to upper division and graduate work until such time as adequate junior college opportunities are provided for the primary area served by these institutions."[6]

Without going into detail about the number and location of new state colleges, it is important to note for present purposes (1) that the design of the Master Plan for Higher Education in California was based on projected college enrollments in 1965, 1970, and 1975; (2) that minimum, optimum, and maximum enrollments were set for each type of higher institution — junior college, state college, state university; (3) that admission requirements for the state colleges and the state university were set at a level that would divert large numbers of high school graduates to an expanded system of junior colleges; (4) that new state colleges and/or campuses of the state university were to be established to accommodate those students eligible for admission to these

[5]*The Master Plan for Higher Education, California* (Sacramento, California: California State Department of Education, 1960), p. 44.

[6]*Ibid*, p. 111.

*The Coordinating Council for Higher Education appointed since this statement was published has assumed some functions that were assigned to the Liaison Committee.

26

institutions for whom facilities would not be available. Taking these factors into account, the Master Plan Survey Team recommended the establishment of 21 new junior colleges, five new state colleges, and certain new campuses of the University to be based on further studies of the magnitude of need.

Study commissions in some states that have employed the usual criteria of projected college enrollments, manpower requirements, and potential capacity of existing institutions are in agreement with the findings in the state of New York that proposed expansion and better utilization of present facilities will provide enough places for all full-time students who seek admission.

The needs for new public senior colleges then are as a rule derived from comprehensive studies made by state boards, councils, or commissions. The factors considered with varying degrees of emphasis are: projected college enrollments, technical and professional manpower needs, maximal projected capacities of existing institutions — public and private, and the location of existing institutions in relation to growing centers of population.

The needs for new private senior colleges, both independent and church-related, generally are less explicitly defined. They are usually expressed in terms of church interest or social needs. Sometimes, in fact more often than might seem to be justified, the impetus for their establishment originates in a local community as an expression of ambition for community advancement and of faith in the merits of a college as a community asset. A few exceptions to these procedures are found in the case of church boards or private agencies that have systematically studied the needs for new colleges.

An illustration of this more objective approach appears in a survey report that led to the establishment of Florida Presbyterian College. The report contains extensive demographic data, estimates of the number of high school graduates in Florida, in- and out-of-state migration of college students, college enrollments at the time of the study and projected enrollments to 1970 of Florida residents, growth of the membership of the Presbyterian group, income and contributions of Presbyterians, and other relevant data. After analyzing the data and conferring with key persons — educators and laymen — the committee that made the study concluded that by establishing a new Presbyterian college,

— The Presbyterian Church would help take care of some portion of the 46 percent increase in college-age youth in Florida who are likely to enter college between 1956 and 1970.

— Another yardstick would be provided in the state of Florida to flank publicly supported colleges and universities.

— Another opportunity for young people to study in an institution free to foster Christian values would be provided.

— The college would stress the liberal arts including simultaneous emphasis on religious faith and critical inquiry.

— More young people would tend to dedicate their lives full time to church vocations — the ministry, religious education, missionary work, etc.

— All students attending such a college would be impregnated with religious spirit because of dedicated faculty members, subject matter related to Christian values, chapel services and other student religious activities, all resulting in the sort of wholesome concern of these young people to determine how they can best express their sense of Christian vocation whether in a lay or professional position.

— For the nation as a whole, another bulwark against materialism and secularism would exist.

— Another church-related institution would be turning out graduates from which society as a whole, as well as the church, will draw its leaders.

— Not just another liberal arts college would be established, but one planned with imagination and vision to settle some of the urgent and critical problems in American life and education.

STEPS IN ESTABLISHING A NEW COLLEGE

Once the need for a new senior college has been determined, the successive steps that must be taken for the orderly development of plans are: (1) securement of legal authorization; (2) organization of a governing board in conformity with the provisions of the charter or articles of incorporation; (3) arrangement for a planning body; and (4) formulation of a design for the college embodying such factors as purposes, size, plan of organization, program pattern and emphases, distinctive characteristics, and physical facilities.

The legal procedures for the establishment of a new college differ widely from one state to another. It is incumbent upon those who are designated to take this first step to ascertain and conform to the legal requirements prescribed by the state in which the college is to be located.

The composition and role of the governing board is a matter of major importance. Generally boards responsible for the government or coordination of state colleges and universities, either on a statewide or an institutional basis, should be relatively small. Actually the size of board membership ranges from three to 102. The average membership for state boards of various types, excluding the exceptionally large board of 102, is 10.6 members. While it cannot be assumed that average size is the best size, observations on administration seem to agree that approximately nine members is a desirable size for optimum effectiveness. The prevailing practice in state institutions is appointment of board members by the governor, usually with the concurrence or approval of the senate, for overlapping terms. A desirable length for each term is six to nine years.

The size, composition, and functions of governing boards of private colleges are determined by those who draft the articles of incorporation. Because there is no validated pattern for the organization of private college boards, there is a great variation among them. There is an emerging consensus, however, among those who are concerned with the administration of private higher education that the boards of private colleges, like those of public institutions, should be comparatively small. One justification of large boards, of twenty-five to forty members, at private colleges is the possibility of wide contacts with the supporting constituency. Generally, however, the actual business of a large board is transacted by an executive committee or some other smaller unit of the whole board.

The functions commonly attributed to boards of trustees for higher institutions, public or private, are very similar. It should be borne in mind in considering the most important of these functions that some may have particular relevance to public institutions, others to private institutions. In brief these functions are:

— to assume responsibility for the establishment and operation of a college in accordance with legal authorization;

— to appoint chief administrative officers of the institution and to approve faculty appointments involving tenure;

— to review and approve policies for the management and operation of the institution;

— to act on recommendations presented by the chief administrative officer and the faculty pertaining to such matters as admission requirements, programs, degrees, plant development, and budget;

— to interpret the purposes and programs of the institution to its constituency and to ascertain and interpret the thinking of the constituency concerning institutional policies, facilities, and programs;

— to evaluate the institution's operational effectiveness;

29

— to appraise the financial needs of the institution;

— to approve the budget and to aid in securing necessary financial support;

— to make periodic reports to the agency — legislature or the denominational body — under whose auspices the institution operates.

These two preliminary steps — securing the legal authorization for a college and the organization of a governing board — lead directly to the serious business of planning the new institution. This is such a far-reaching and important step that it demands the contributions of the most informed, imaginative, and resourceful minds that can be enlisted in the endeavor. The approaches to planning a new college embody two basic patterns: (1) a planning commission made up of distinguished educators operating under the leadership of a director; (2) the president of the new college and key staff members operating with the assistance of professional consultants.

Other things being equal, the latter plan is to be preferred. There are circumstances, however, when this approach is not feasible. Such was the case in planning what has become Florida Atlantic University. In this instance the establishment of the new institution was authorized by the legislature, but there were funds available only for planning purposes. The Board of Control was confronted with the alternative of appointing an *ad hoc* planning commission or delaying all planning until the legislature made further appropriations to permit the appointment of the nucleus of a permanent staff. The Board chose the former course. It first enlisted the services of a distinguished educational leader to confer with key people throughout the country to elicit suggestions of the most forward-looking ideas that might be incorporated into a new college program. On the basis of this exploratory survey, a draft of a prospectus for the new college was prepared.

The next step was a critical appraisal of the ideas contained in the prospectus. For this purpose, a planning commission was appointed with a full-time director and a small professional and secretarial staff. An advisory committee of seven nationally known educators was appointed to assist the director of the commission. The advisory committee met in five two-day sessions over a period of six months. A number of resource persons, including representatives of several firms of architects, participated in these planning sessions. For the purpose of studying intensively specific aspects of the evolving plan, a task force was appointed in each of the following areas: television and other media; testing; student personnel services; and library. Special conferences were also held to consider such subjects as teacher education; the organization of the sciences, the humanities and the social sciences; and space requirements.

In contrast to this procedure was the plan followed in the development of the University of South Florida which was also initially conceived as a state college organized under the same Board of Control as Florida Atlantic. In this case, enough funds were appropriated by the legislature to enable the Board to appoint the president and key supporting personnel to whom was delegated responsibility for all phases of planning excepting the selection of a site which already had been determined by the Board. The president, with the aid of a small staff and a number of consultants, developed a comprehensive design for the new institution.

Still another approach to planning is that followed in drafting a design for Hampshire College in Massachusetts. This was a joint venture of three private colleges — Amherst, Mount Holyoke, Smith — and the state University of Massachusetts.

The presidents of the four cooperating institutions appointed a committee of four — one member from each institution — "to develop the plans for a new experimental college aimed at producing education of the highest quality at a minimum cost per student and with as small a faculty relative to the size of the student body as new methods of instruction and new administrative procedures can make possible." The committee was given its assignment on May 6, 1958, and on November 14, of the same year, it submitted its report to the four presidents. Details of procedure are not given in the report, but there is an acknowledgement of the assistance of more than 50 faculty and staff members of the cooperating institutions and of 26 outside consultants. The plans presented by the committee with further review and revision provide the basic concepts for Hampshire College.

These few illustrations do not cover all approaches to effective planning. They suffice, however, to emphasize the importance of an orderly procedure by imaginative and wise personnel who rely heavily on the counsel and criticism of specialists.

Both observations and personal experience suggest that an essential factor in planning is continuity. This can be achieved most effectively by delegating responsibility for planning to those who will be expected to carry out the plans, namely the president and his supporting staff. This approach requires that the governing board have a special concern for selecting key persons whose

31

experience and educational outlook is broad, imaginative, and creative.

Selecting Personnel Required for Effective Planning and Operation

The appointment of the president of a new college is a crucial step, because within the framework of a statement of purposes and policies adopted by the board, he is the architect of the new college. He is not bound by traditions that have crystallized over many years nor by a well entrenched curriculum, faculty or pattern of organization, or by concerned alumni or unconcerned students.

This appointment should be made as soon as the board feels assured that both the need for the institution and the requisite resources for its support justify going ahead. The literature on how to proceed in choosing a president and on his responsibilities provides background information and suggestions of procedure that are far too comprehensive to be summarized here. Some of these sources are listed in the bibliography of this brochure.

Several facts are of such importance, however, that they must be noted.

It will be necessary for the board to identify as explicitly as it can the combination of qualifications it considers essential. These will differ, depending on the kind of institution envisaged, whether it is to be a publicly supported liberal arts college, whether it is to be a church-related college intended to serve a particular denominational constituency, or whether it is to be a forward-looking private, independent college.

As one reads analyses and descriptions of the essential characteristics of college presidents, he is inevitably impressed with the recurrence of certain traits. A mere notation of some of them will give an idea of what a paragon of virtues a college president is expected to be.

— He must be a scholar of such standing as to command the respect of his colleagues.

— He must be fired by deep concern for education.

— He must be able to set the tone and quality of the institution.

— He will personify the institution and must, therefore, be able to create a favorable public image.

— He must have courage to make unpopular decisions.

32

— He must be able to exercise leadership in a situation involving diverse and often conflicting interests.

— He must be a man of action, but action not by the exercise of force but of consultation and persuasion on the basis of facts.

— He must have patience in gaining faculty support in his efforts to advance the institution.

— He must prevent desirable tension from degenerating into "rancorous and damaging strife."

— He must avoid a policy of "peace at any price" that results in "the sterility of one big, dull, happy family."

— He must have a clearly formulated and enunciated philosophy of education expressed in clarity of goals.

— He must cultivate divine discontent with the *status quo.*

— He must have a firm commitment to important values — values that are compatible with those of the college constituency.

— He must not be so youthful as to give the impression of immaturity and inexperience, nor so advanced in years to give the impression that he is likely to be out of step with the rapidly changing times.

— He must be able to delegate responsibility and commensurate authority.

—He must be able to communicate effectively with faculty and students and with the public.

— He must have a nervous constitution which will enable him to live habitually at a focal point of conflicting pressures.

The masculine pronoun is used in the generic sense in these statements. It is not to be construed as excluding women from consideration.

Since no potential president will possess all of these qualifications in equal degree or even at all in some instances, the board of trustees or other responsible agency will have to decide which ones are of paramount importance for the position to be filled. Then it must make a diligent search for the best qualified candidates. It should consult officers of educational organizations —

national and regional, administrative officers of other colleges and universities, foundation officers, and leading businessmen and women who are members of other boards of trustees or otherwise connected with higher institutions. Once a preliminary list of promising personnel has been made, it should undergo rigid screening to identify the two or three most likely possibilities. Further screening must be made on the basis of personal interviews. Never should a board fall into the error of being unduly influenced by the personal connections or preferences of an individual board member. Though it may be difficult to arrive at a unanimous decision, there should be agreement by a substantial majority of the board; otherwise, a new president will have two strikes against him before he starts.

The person elected to the presidency of a new college, if the board has followed a sound procedure, has a right to feel highly complimented; but he should not be unduly influenced by this tribute in arriving at a decision. There are a number of conditions that might make the position unacceptable to him, though it might be quite acceptable to another person. Some of the specific considerations he should take into account are: why he was elected for the position — what qualifications were given the greatest weight, e.g., his distinction as a scholar-educator; his prominence as a church leader or a public figure; or previous success as an administrator. Also to be considered are the reasons for establishing the college — demographic, political, philosophical, religious; commitments already made by the legislature, the church body, the board or other agency regarding policies or staff personnel.

These suggestions may appear to be gratuitous. The justification for including them is the number of instances that can be cited in which new college presidents found themselves in deep, hot water because they failed to make a thorough advance appraisal of the situation.

Assuming that the president is duly appointed, what are his next steps? He will have to move in several directions simultaneously. To do this effectively will require the determination of certain administrative priorities; otherwise, he will be headed for academic schizophrenia. Unless location and site have already been decided upon, this will be one major concern; he will also need to outline a plan of administrative organization for which key personnel will have to be employed at an early date; the development of the educational program, the heart of the new college, will require thoughtful direction; and the design of physical facilities adapted functionally to the requirements of the program will be a pressing matter. In addition, the news media and the general public will be clamoring for information about plans in progress. Speaking engagements, press releases, correspondence, conferences with school administrators and with legislators, if it is a public college, or with constituents and with prospective donors, if it is private — these are activities that cannot be ignored, time consuming as they may be.

The time allowed for the institution to become operative is another factor that has an important bearing on the ordering of these multiple demands. Usually too little time is allowed; consequently, as the time for opening approaches, pressures mount and activities become frenzied. An examination of the sequence of events in the establishment of a number of new colleges suggests that at least two years should be allowed from issuance of a charter to the admission of the first class. In some instances this period is extended to four or five years. Much depends upon what must be done during this time, but general observation indicates that a period of two years is too short for the most satisfactory, unhurried development of a new college.

Without attempting to establish any order of relative importance, the several areas of administrative responsibility and their interrelationships need to be considered further.

In evolving an appropriate administrative pattern, it is necessary to identify the functions, the things that must be done. Once identified, those functions most closely related can be grouped and assigned to an administrative unit. There are, for example, such functions as the formulation of specific objectives consistent with the general purposes of the college; the organization of an educational program designed to aid in achieving the educational objectives; the formulation of conditions of faculty service that make teaching in the college attractive; the identification of teachers qualified to direct the educational program; the interpretation to the faculty of institutional purposes and policies; the development of improved teaching procedures and improved methods of measuring the educational progress and achievement of students; the definition of admission and graduation requirements; a continual appraisal of the effectiveness of the educational operation; the presentation of recommendations to the president on such matters as promotion, tenure, salaries; the formulation of financial requirements that constitute the basis for budget requests. All of these functions have to do with the conduct and quality of the academic program. They may, therefore, be allocated to a chief academic administrative officer for whom the title "academic dean" is especially appropriate.

Other areas of administrative responsibility when similarly analyzed will indicate the need for an office in which are centered functions relating to the financial affairs and the management of the physical facilities; an office in which are centered all functions pertaining to students including such matters as admissions, testing and counseling, financial aid, the social and educational aspects of housing, health services, records and reports, placement, recreation, student organizations and activities, and government; another office for public relations responsibilities for effective liaison with the constituency — legislative, church, or general public — is also called for. The titles for the incumbents of these several offices should identify their respective functional spheres, but titles are less important than the clear delineation of the functions of each office. But no matter how clearly the functional spheres of officers may be defined, there will inevitably arise situations that will call for an arbitrary allocation of a responsibility to one office or another. The president must be the key person in this organization whatever the pattern. Even though he delegates large responsibility and commensurate authority to his supporting administrators, he will still have to make many final decisions. If he becomes deeply involved in money-raising, plant planning, and essential extramural activities, he may need an administrative assistant to keep him up to date on campus affairs and to provide him with facts essential to intelligent action.

Below this top level of administrative officers will be additional personnel whose functions will be determined by the pattern of organization. For example, if the curriculum is organized along departmental lines, department heads may be called for; if the curriculum conforms to newer patterns of organization, division heads or other appropriate officers may be indicated. In any event, the functions to be performed and the personnel required should be determined by the top echelon administrative officers in consultation with the president once they have been appointed.

Two principles of administrative organization and procedure need to be emphasized at this point. First, levels of administrative personnel imply a hierarchy. There must, of necessity, be a hierarchy of organization, but there must nevertheless be democracy in operation. Administration by consensus rather than by fiat is essential to high morale and cooperative endeavor. Many occasions will arise, however, when full accord cannot be reached. It then becomes necessary for the responsible officer to make a decision. Second, the very nature of administrative organization, the allocation of functions accompanied by authority to make decisions, tends to compartmentalize operations and to create barriers to communication. It is exceedingly important, therefore, that channels of two-way communication among administrative officers and from administrative officers to board members, faculty members, students, and constituents be established and kept open by regular use.

In emphasizing the importance of communication Woodburne says:

> One of the first conditions of effective college or university administration is the existence of two-way communication between the various officers and staff members. The advantages, in fact a necessity, of two-way communication are manifest, although this process constitutes a blind spot in many educational institutions . . . . Effective two-way communication requires that all persons whose interests are vitally affected by a proposal be able to participate in the discussions from the time the problem is defined until a final decision is reached.[7]

More needs to be said about the selection of key administrative personnel. It is urgent that top level administrative positions be filled as soon as qualified appointees can be found. Of highest priority are the chief academic administrator — academic dean or vice president for academic affairs — and the officer responsible for business and financial affairs. The academic dean is central to the development of the educational program and plans for instruction which are basic to the projection of faculty needs and physical plant requirements. The early appointment of the chief business and financial officer is important, too, because an accounting and budgeting system must be developed, funds and payrolls must be administered, and physical facilities or properties that may be acquired must be supervised. The time of appointment of a public relations officer and of a dean of students will be determined by the point at which the need for their services becomes apparent. Certainly the dean of students should be directly involved in setting up admissions procedures, plans for student housing, the determination of the kinds of services — counseling, health, financial, recreational — that will be provided, and the provision of essential record forms.

The new president must engage in a search for an academic dean comparable to the search made by the trustees to find a president. He must have a clearly formulated job description both to guide him in his search and to interpret the position to the prospective candidate.

---

[7]Lloyd S. Woodburne, *Principles of College and University Administration* (Stanford, California: Stanford University Press, 1958), p. 16.

Once the academic dean or vice president is appointed, the next important step is the appointment of key faculty personnel. The number and subject matter areas they represent will depend on the educational philosophy expressed in the purposes of the college. At the very least there should be one scientist, one social scientist, and one representative of the humanities. These should be top level scholars whose perspective is broad.

In association with the dean, these appointees should constitute an educational council dedicated to the development of the instructional program and procedures. As soon as the pattern of the program is agreed upon and the plan of instruction has been formulated, it will be necessary to project further faculty needs at successive stages in the institution's development.

Of special importance in planning the educational program is the role of the library. No matter how its role is defined, steps must be initiated as early as possible for securing books, publications, recordings, and instructional material and for accessioning them. This means that the librarian should be among the first appointments made by the dean and should be a member of the educational council.

The educational council will also need individual consultants on specific aspects of the program, and it should have an ongoing advisory committee of distinguished educators to whom it can look for exciting new ideas and who may serve as a sounding board for ideas the council itself may generate.

The educational council and its advisory body should proceed on the theory that physical facilities will be designed to serve the purposes and functions of program rather than to control them. With this fact in mind, representatives of architectural firms that are interested in participating in designing and constructing physical facilities should be invited to attend planning sessions so that they may be oriented to the point of view expressed in the program and in proposed methods of instruction. The importance of this participation by architects may be seen in terms of the library. The library has been conceived in conventional terms as a place where books are kept and where students go to use them, but library services are coming to be more broadly defined in terms of a wide range of learning resources such as individual study carrels equipped with cybernetic devices that put a variety of kinds of information at the student's fingertips, programmed learning resources, language laboratory equipment, visual instructional materials, music recordings and listening rooms, art files, and other types of learning aids. Obviously a design of such a learning resources center will differ markedly from the conventional library.

The subject of conditions that affect physical facilities is considered more fully in a later section. The point here is that to design buildings for educational functions, architects must be thoroughly oriented to the functions to be served. The importance of non-professional personnel must not be overlooked. Excellent secretarial and clerical services can save untold man-hours of professional administrative time. It is poor economy for professors laboriously or even skillfully to type their own letters, examinations, reports, and manuscripts or to spend time in classifying and filing materials. It is equally important to provide competent assistants and stock room clerks, operators of computers, and managers and operators of duplicating services. From the earliest stages of planning, the adequacy of non-professional services should be a matter of continuing concern.

From the quality of personnel — from the president to the custodian — will derive the excellence of a new college, public or private. From the nature of the program and the methods of directing learning will derive the distinctive character of the institution.

While both programs and methods must evolve during the process of planning, it is not inappropriate to suggest some special considerations that merit attention.

Determining Purposes

The first questions to be considered by a planning committee or commission are what kind of college is needed, what are to be its controlling and guiding purposes, what is its mission. José Ortega y Gasset identifies the starting point in these words:

> But an institution cannot be built of wholesome usage until its precise mission has been determined. An institution is a machine in that its whole structure and functioning must be designed in view of the service it is expected to perform. In other words, the root of university reform is a complete formulation of its purpose. Any alteration or touching up or adjustment about this house of ours unless it starts by reviewing the problem of its mission—clearly, decisively, truthfully—will be love's labor lost.[8]

The mission of a new college is, of course, to serve a demonstrated educational need. This generalization must, however, be translated into more specific terms. The kind of institution envisaged will be reflected in the purposes it is designed to serve,

[8]José Ortega y Gasset, *Mission of the University* (Princeton, N. J.: Princeton University Press, 1944), pp. 46-47, quoted in *Improving College and University Teaching*, XI (Autumn, 1963), p. 219.

the distinctive ways in which it will fulfill its purposes, the size and pattern of organization that will be most appropriate to its effective operation, the scope and organization of its program, and the innovations that may be introduced. There is no blueprint for a new college that embodies all of these elements. In fact, such a blueprint would be a disservice because to impose or even to suggest a standard pattern would impair the diversity of institutions, one of the sources of strength in higher education in the United States.

Although each new college should have its own well formulated statement of purposes, it still is possible to profit by certain general principles that have been derived from experience and by an examination of published statements of purposes and programs. Dressel notes, for example, that institutional purposes must be reasonable in number; consistent with one another; of the same level of generality or specificity; distinctive, but not completely independent; and verifiably achievable.[9] Generally, purposes should be expressed in behavioral terms — terms that provide the basis for evaluating student progress and achievement. Some statements of purposes are so general as to be meaningless for program planning and for assessing student achievement, while others are so specific that they are overly restrictive. In arriving at a statement of purposes, consideration should be given to such issues as these: the student constituency for whom the program is designed, the kind and depth of knowledge students should acquire, the intellectual habits and skills students should develop, the provision of a common cultural experience for students of different cultural backgrounds, the emphasis to be given to religion and ethics, the incorporation of an essential degree of flexibility.

Statements made by two institutions — one publicly supported, the other private church related — while not presented as models, will illustrate what appear to be well thought out purposes.

The report of the planning commission of a publicly supported institution contains the following statement of purpose:

1. *To develop as fully as possible the intellectual power of each student.* In working with students toward this objective, it will be the purpose of the university to develop: (1) intellectual competence in thinking, reasoning, evaluating; (2) the abilities to read, write, speak, watch, listen; (3) the motivation and skills for independent learning; and (4) abilities and interest in creative expression.

[9]Paul L. Dressel, *et al.*, *Evaluation in Higher Education* (Boston: Houghton Mifflin Co., 1961).

2. *To aid students to acquire significant knowledge and the ability to relate it to great issues in a rapidly changing world.* Here it will be the aim of the program to acquaint the student with: (1) the role of human need and cultural values in environmental change; (2) the role of leadership in effecting environmental change; (3) the arts and humanities as forces in environmental change; (4) the value and use of scientific methods in developing the theory and practice of organization and administration; (5) research as a tool of administration; (6) comparative cultural systems and their effect on administrative techniques in business, government, etc.; and (7) the effect of biological, physical, and cultural factors on the individual, community, and larger national and international groupings. This list is not intended to prescribe limits, but rather to suggest emphases pertinent to all parts of the total program.

3. *To aid students to acquire the ability to pursue intensively a limited area of knowledge.* This will require the ability to employ techniques of criticism and research appropriate to the area of concentration. The full achievement of this objective should give the student a sense of being a scholar in his field of special interest.

4. *To aid students to acquire knowledge, abilities, and skills that are relevant to their educational interest and goals.* The chief emphasis will be placed on principles and their practical application. This approach is based on an assumption that specific techniques can be acquired best in some form of internship experience. Such practical experiences may be combined with the student's program or may be postponed until later.

5. *To aid students to develop individual value patterns that are basic to sound decisions and actions in a free society.* One phase of this objective can be achieved by aiding the student to understand his possible role in a changing world so that he may define realistically his own life goals.[10]

The corresponding statement of purposes adopted by the faculty of a private church-related college is:

1. To understand the common phenomena in one's physical and biological environment, to apply habits of scientific thought to both personal and civic problems, and to appreciate the implications of scientific discoveries for human welfare.

2. To participate actively as an informed and responsible citizen in meeting the social, economic, and political problems of one's community, State, and Nation.

3. To understand the ideas of others and to express one's own effectively (communication).

---

[10]"Report of the Planning Commission for a New University at Boca Raton," (Tallahassee, Florida: Board of Regents, 1961), pp. 5-7 (Mimeographed).

4. To recognize the interdependence of the different peoples of the world and one's personal responsibility for fostering international understanding and peace.

5. To understand and enjoy literature, art, music, and other cultural activities as expressions of personal and social experience.

6. To develop for the regulation of one's personal and civic life a code of behavior based on Christian principles and democratic ideals.[11]

One phase of these objectives relates to the acquisition of discriminating value judgments — critical taste — in literature and the arts. There is an almost overwhelming flood of productions of such varying characteristics and quality as to be utterly confusing to the unsophisticated. If higher education can do nothing more than aid the individual to identify qualities in literature and the arts that justify his appreciation of them, it will have gone beyond what most higher education does. Also, the kind of value pattern that a student acquires has a special relevance in the area of ethics and religion. Studies of the impact of college and university education on the attitudes and value patterns of students indicate that the total effect is limited or negligible. Moral action should find a justification beyond social sanction. One of the important outcomes of college experience should be an individual's justification of his standard of ethical behavior.

Once the purposes of a new college have been formulated, a program appropriate to the achievement of the purposes must be designed.

The design should incorporate the best elements of conventional programs and new ideas derived from innovation and experimentation currently in effect in pioneering colleges. Conventional programs are of many types and patterns, some up-to-date and forward-looking, others out-moded looking to the past. A new college whose purposes are oriented to the present and future should derive its ideas from institutions that are up-to-date and forward-looking. It cannot afford to replicate a program that harks back to earlier times, no matter how outstanding it may have been.

While up-to-date conventional college programs are important sources of ideas for a new college, it is unnecessary to undertake

[11]*Casebook on Campus Planning and Institutional Development: Ten Institutions: How They Did It*, compiled by John B. Rork and Leslie F. Robbins, U.S. Office of Education Circular No. 667 (Washington, D.C.: U.S. Government Printing Office, 1962), pp. 99-100.

to identify here such programs that might be replicated in whole or in part.

There are, however, innovations about which information is less readily available that may contribute to the distinctiveness of new colleges. A few examples from particular institutions followed by a summary of departures from conventional procedures found in a number of colleges will suggest ideas for consideration in the development of a new college program.

One college has developed a program that frees students and faculty from the usual plan of giving and taking courses to cover specific subjects. Students choose from areas of learning those that are especially related to their goals. Their achievement is tested by comprehensive examinations. The total offering of lecture courses is small but these offerings may be supplemented by course offerings in other institutions. A month long mid-winter term will be devoted to a common college-wide study of two courses; one centered on Western Culture, the other on non-Western Culture.

Another new college stresses the mastery of a small number of really vital ideas, principles and modes of analysis. Out of the educational experience in this college the student is expected to derive an appreciation for the unity of knowledge.

To achieve this unity through program organization, the curriculum is divided into three broad divisions — the natural sciences, the social sciences, and the humanities. Primary responsibility for his education rests on the student. Accordingly, there is a large degree of flexibility in the program and student progress is based on demonstrated competence and mastery of an area of knowledge. This essential degree of flexibility is incompatible with the usual classifications of students by years, freshman, sophomore, junior, senior. Three broad categories or levels of achievement are established, but a student may be working simultaneously at different levels depending on his demonstrated competence.

Level I covers the three areas of subject matter comprising basic or general education, namely the social sciences, the natural sciences, and the humanities. On Level II, the student spends about two-thirds of his time in exploring in depth areas of special interest and about one-third in electives or in further extension of his general education. At Level III, the student's time is divided approximately evenly between an advanced seminar and individual project work on the one hand, and participation in an interdisciplinary seminar designed to achieve an integration in the major fields of knowledge on the other hand.

Another comparatively new college, one that admitted its first class in 1960, has incorporated several innovations. In this instance, as in the preceding case, it is difficult to separate program from process. The primary emphasis is placed on independent study. The conditions adopted to make the program effective were the selection of better-than-average students; the selection of a highly competent faculty interested in experimenting in independent study; the elimination of required class attendance, required chapel attendance, the grade point system; faculty involvement in student government and student disciplinary matters; a reading proficiency requirement; an open-stack library; an open-door classroom policy that permits a student to sit in on any lecture of an instructor; an inter-semester winter term of independent study for all students; opportunities to make up deficiencies or to demonstrate advanced achievement by comprehensive examinations; the establishment of a core program which provides a common experience for all students; the preparation of a projected program of studies by each student near the close of his first year; introduction of a student instructor program in which the most highly capable juniors and seniors are employed to assist professors in their teaching and research activities. Each of these items could be expanded at considerable length, but this summary will give an idea of the nature and scope of the innovations at this college.

Still other departures from conventional procedures are found in new colleges. Without going into further detail, however, these departures are incorporated into the following summary of distinctive characteristics.

— Related fields of knowledge are welded together with minimal consideration of departmental organization thereby giving students an understanding and appreciation of the unity of knowledge.

— Important new ideas of knowledge are incorporated into the program. Some of these developments represent information derived from the rapidly expanding frontiers of knowledge. Some represent previously neglected areas of human civilization and culture.

— Some new programs stress the importance of being highly selective in terms of the content of the educational program on the theory that a limited amount of knowledge well taught is far more valuable than an attempt to cover superficially large areas.

— Degree requirements are defined by areas of educational experience related to individual interests and objectives. The rate of student progress in the fulfillment of degree requirements is determined by individual ability. Requirements may be fulfilled by comprehensive examination based on independent study. This places the primary responsibility for the student's education upon the student himself.

— Credit hours, grade points, time requirements are abandoned and the usual class structure — freshman, sophomore, junior, senior — disappears.

— In the admission of students, increasing emphasis is placed upon evidence of ability, achievement, maturity with less weight given to such matters as average grades in high school and rank in class, or even the results of some of the usual admissions examinations.

— The essence of instruction is the confrontation of first-class minds. This point of view leads to an examination of the validity of hypotheses concerning teaching and learning. It also leads to an evaluation of the role of new media of instruction in the process of teaching and learning. For example, plans are in the making for the confrontation of first-class minds on an international basis by the use of international telecasts. Experiments are also under way with individual study carrels where students can have immediately at their command a wide range of recordings and visual aids.

— In a few institutions the educational program begins at the junior year on the premise that basic education will be provided by junior colleges.

— A campus on board a ship combines classroom instruction with education tours and with special projects in ports of call.

— The library is the focus of the educational program. In addition to books and pamphlets, it provides microfilm materials, slides, and films with appropriate projection rooms and equipment, music recordings and listening rooms, exhibits of original and reproductions of works of art. Associated with the library in what is designated as a learning resources center are language laboratories, programmed learning, audio-visual aids, and testing and counseling services.

— To facilitate the progress of students and to make maximal use of facilities, programs operate on a year-round basis.

— An extended inter-term period is provided for independent study and work on special projects.

— Clinical and counseling services are provided to aid students in identifying weaknesses in their preparation or limitations in their abilities, to appraise aptitudes and interests, and to aid in planning programs.

— The advantages of the small college will be provided either by limiting enrollments to 1200-1500 students or, in an institution of a large projected enrollment, providing for separate colleges with distinctive programs with small enrollments.

The purpose in presenting this somewhat comprehensive resumé of innovations is to suggest that a new college must be conceived in the perspective of new developments in higher education designed to keep abreast of social change.

Planning an Educational Program

Those responsible for planning the educational program of a new college are in an enviable though difficult position. Their position is enviable because they are free from the pressures and resistances of faculty and alumni that are commonly encountered in efforts to reform an established curriculum. They are in a difficult position because current developments in higher education suggest so many new ideas that must be weighed and so many directions in which they might go. Most important is the fact that the undergraduate college curriculum is not static; to keep in step with the enormously expanding fields of knowledge and with the unprecedented social changes in which we are both participants and beneficiaries, the curriculum must undergo constant renewal.

A special consideration in planning a curriculum is the diversity that characterizes our higher education. Some countries that have centralized control of higher education also have uniform programs. The matter of diversity, therefore, presents little in the way of a problem for them. In the United States, however, distinctive purposes and programs, distinctive procedures, and distinctive facilities are inherent elements in planning developments in colleges and universities, old and new. It is not to the discredit of a new college, if, in its efforts to relate its program realistically to individual and social needs, it adopts a program that has many elements in common with those of other colleges that have engaged in a like analytical procedure. The important point is that it should not be a program borrowed uncritically from another institution.

Both the facts of accelerated social change and of institutional individuality make it impracticable to present a proposed model curriculum. It is important, however, in planning a curriculum to have clearly in mind certain basic factors and concepts.

Some of the important factors to be considered are:

1. The objectives of the educational program must be consonant with the purposes for which the college is being established.

2. The focus of the educational program is the student. The characteristics and needs of the students to be educated must be envisaged. What will be their educational and social background? Will they come primarily from a church constituency or from a broader social milieu? Will the student body be coeducational or of a single sex? Will the student body be primarily residential or commuting, or a combination of both? Will a considerable number of students have to work part time? Will special provisions be made for married students with families?

3. The objectives of the program should be expressed in terms of expected outcomes, that is, the changes that occur in students during their college experience. The anticipated outcome should be conceived in terms of knowledge, understandings, abilities and skills, attitudes, habits — all related to the role of the individual in a changing society.

4. Concepts of the learning process and conditions affecting learning must be clearly defined. This will involve such matters as the amount of responsibility that will be placed on the student; provisions for differential rates of progress of students in terms of ability and previous preparation; the role of the faculty in motivating and directing learning; the use that will be made of instructional aids — television, programmed learning, language laboratories, recordings and slides; provisions that will be made for first-hand experience, for example, combination work and study, intersession em-

ployment or travel, study abroad; and the methods that will be used for evaluating student progress and achievement.

5. The question of cost will affect plans for curriculum and instruction. Costs are determined by the plan of organization of the program, by the use of automation, by the role of the faculty, in fact, by all of the elements affecting learning already noted.

There are also some more specific concepts that have an important bearing on curriculum development. The following are of particular relevance and importance:

1. *The issue of breadth and depth is one of primary concern.*

The question is how to provide a good general education and also adequate opportunity for specialization. For years definitions of general education and specialization have been cast in terms of required courses, majors and credit hours. This somewhat arbitrary distinction between general education and specialization fades out when both are comprehended in the term "liberal education." Liberal education as characterized by the late William de Vane, former dean at Yale, "Should inculate a point of view, a sense of perspective and tolerance, a breadth of sympathy, and ability to see the relationships of things in balance and proportion."[12] Thus conceived, the educational program that produces the liberally educated person must be designed in terms of both breadth and depth without arbitrary distinction between the two.

2. *As to content, limits must be set on the scope of the program because it is no longer possible to cover within a reasonable length of time all major fields of knowledge.*

Some principles of selection must, therefore, be employed. One commonly used is that the student should have an intellectual experience in representative areas of knowledge, for example, the humanities, the social sciences, the natural sciences; also, that he should go more deeply into one area. The conventional provision for the deeper penetration has been the departmental major, but new and more imaginative substitutes for departmental majors must be sought.

One approach to this problem is illustrated by a plan recently introduced at Beloit College. The new approach is described, in part, as follows:

---

[12]William C. de Vane, "A Time and Place for Liberal Education," *Liberal Education*, (May, 1964), p. 209.

Requiring the student to take courses in diverse academic disciplines in order to achieve breadth in education will now be abandoned. In its place each student will be required to prepare for and to pass comprehensive examinations in each of the three major areas of knowledge: social science, natural science, and the humanities. The student will have far more choice and responsibility than heretofore in choosing his own means of achieving such competencies: independent reading, auditing of courses, taking courses for credit, reviewing quality, high school courses in his background, etc.

Each student will be expected to spend at least one term in an off-campus field term, either in the United States or abroad, devoted to college-related work, study, social service, field work, research, or any combination thereof. The possibility for variation of the student's nine-term program will be great; and he may under certain conditions combine his field term with one or even two vacation terms, thus achieving as much as a three-term period of unbroken field experience.[13]

3. *Inherent in the concept of liberal education is the provision for new fields of knowledge and for the inclusion of non-Western cultures.*

The frontiers of knowledge are expanding so rapidly that large segments of knowledge become obsolete and must, therefore, be replaced by up-to-date information. The implications of this fact are twofold: first, plans for a college curriculum must have built-in provisions for continuous revision; second, knowledge is in a constant state of change and major emphasis should be placed on methods of inquiry, of analytical thinking, of evaluating, and of effective use of source information.

We are becoming increasingly aware of the great — one is almost tempted to say, tragic — omission of significant segments of human culture in our college programs. There is a growing recognition, for example, of the need for much greater emphasis on the cultures of the Middle East, and the Orient and Latin America. Our citizens, whether professional, diplomatic or lay who have contacts with the people whose culture we have neglected, tend to be poorly informed. They are ignorant because our curricula have highlighted only the history of Western civilization. Dr. Paul Dressel expressed this point of view as follows:

Our ready assumption that Western culture and particularly its later flowering in the United States is superior to other existing

---

[13]Sumner Hayward, "Five Experimental Programs in Undergraduate Liberal Arts," *Current Issues in Higher Education* (Washington, D. C.: Association for Higher Education, 1964), pp. 68-69.

cultures in the world is certainly dubious. Our general ignorance of non-Western cultures is a serious and disabling deficiency which we must soon remedy if we are to understand and be understood and accepted by rapidly developing nations.[14]

Another writer expresses the same point of view in these terms:

> Until all undergraduates get some intelligent exposure to at least one non-Western culture, their education is hardly adequate for a responsible world citizenship. Moreover, they will be denied contact with the wealth, art, experience, and insight of ancient and vital human communities whose very ability to survive and create testifies to their superior resourcefulness and qualities of mind and spirit.[15]

4. *Another unsolved problem with which curriculum planners must grapple is how to inter-relate professional education and the liberal arts.*

Liberal arts colleges have been charged with surrendering their true functions to vocational objectives. In a sense all liberal education has a vocational overtone; if it is designed to enable the individual to live effectively in a free society, it must recognize that finding and fulfilling his place in the world of work is one aspect of effective living. The problem in planning a curriculum is, however, how to achieve an appropriate balance between professional-vocational subject matter and the more general areas. Several observations made by McGrath and Russell, based on a study of trends in the introduction of professional courses, are in point. They say:

> The arresting fact is that the programs in even the most conservative liberal arts colleges have been revolutionized in the past several decades through the addition of programs with specific vocational objectives.[16]

Conversely it should also be noted that professional schools have through the years increased the proportion of the total curriculum devoted to general education, the subjects traditionally classified as the liberal arts and sciences. Professional schools are, moreover, placing more emphasis in their professional programs on principles and less on specific techniques and procedures.

---

[14]Paul L. Dressel, "A Look at New Curriculum Models for Undergraduate Education," *Current Issues in Higher Education* (Washington, D. C.: Association for Higher Education, 1964), p. 144.

[15]Howard A. Reed, "Trends in Non-Western Studies in U.S. Liberal Arts Colleges," *Current Issues in Higher Education* (Washington, D. C.: Association for Higher Education, 1964), p. 179.

[16]Earl J. McGrath and Charles H. Russell, *Are Liberal Arts Colleges Becoming Professional Schools?* (New York: Bureau of Publications, Teachers College, Columbia University, 1958), p. 12.

They are becoming more liberal and less vocational. While trends and current practices do not constitute an adequate guide to the reconciliation of professional and liberal arts emphasis in the development of new college programs, they do suggest approaches that merit consideration.

McGrath and Russell summarize the issues in these words:

> With these protections of their ancient trust, the liberal arts colleges can confidently continue the developments which this study has revealed have been operative since the late nineteenth century. They can and must continue to provide that humane learning and cultivate those intellectual and moral traits which are the only sure guarantee of the continuous health and enrichment of our culture. With this general instruction they can legitimately, as they have been doing, combine courses more closely related to that work of the world which only those who have had specialized education beyond the secondary school can satisfactorily do. Then the liberal arts colleges, together with their sister institutions called the professional schools, will be providing for American youth that generous education which, in the words of Milton, ". . . fits a man to perform justly, skilfully, and magnanimously all the offices, both private and public, of peace and war."[17]

5. *Curriculum planners must face the question of what consideration shall be given to the impact of the student's educational experience on his pattern of values.*

While some studies report that the impact of this college experience on student value patterns is less than what is usually expected, this conclusion serves to intensify rather than minimize the importance of this aspect of the student's college experience. Unless an individual is indifferent to the meaning and direction of his own life and to the conditions affecting him and others, he must make decisions. To make wise decisions he must have a pattern of values — standards by which to weigh the consequences of his actions. The value pattern he brings to college must be tested and redefined in the light of new experience — experience in weighing facts, experience in on- and off-campus group activities, experience in identifying qualities of excellence in literature and the fine arts. Whether the acquisition and revision of value patterns is regarded to be a by-product of the college experience, or whether it is to be a matter of primary concern, is an issue that must be faced. If it is a matter of primary concern, how is it reflected in the curriculum and in the total campus experience?

6. *The concept of time required to complete the educational program is important.*

---

[17]*Ibid.*, p. 26.

Sometimes this is a controlling factor. It enters into planning in several ways. Two points of view are reflected in the following statements. The late Dean William C. de Vane of Yale University observed that:

> The four-year term has remained alive to the present in order to preserve a home for the full-flowering collegiate way of life which we now have so abundantly. The two-or-three-year program of the nineteenth century was often a tacit confession of lack of substance in the curriculum. But there is nothing sacred about the four-year span of college life. What is precious is the achievement by the student of a strong hold upon past and present reality, a quality and a maturity of mind and character—whether such a state be achieved in three years or four, or in some cases even two. There is virtue in a substantial period of time for the leisurely maturing of the character and spirit, but that time will vary from student to student, within certain biological limits.[18]

A counter point of view is expressed by Francis H. Horn as follows:

> The business of the college of arts and sciences—I distinguish this from the business of the university—is the making of men and women. And it can no longer be done, even as imperfectly as institutions of higher education can do it at their best, in the traditional four years, increasingly being compressed into three . . . . The normal undergraduate program should require five years.[19]

Certainly the current trend is toward better use of time and also saving time when it is possible without jeopardizing quality. Evidence of this trend is found in plans for year-round operation, for the use of intersession periods for educational purposes, for fulfillment of requirements by examination, for the early admission of superior students, and for a combination of bachelor's degree and professional degree programs in such fields as law and engineering. In fact, the program requiring five academic years may be quite defensible on philosophical grounds, but appears to be quite unrealistic in the light of current trends, unless it leads to a master's degree.

Selection of Location

One question of paramount importance in the establishment of a new college is where it shall be located. "Where" refers both to the general area in a state or region and to the specific site within that area.

---

[18]William C. de Vane, op. cit., p. 202.

[19]Francis H. Horn, "Forces Shaping the College of Arts and Sciences," *Liberal Education*, L (March, 1964), p. 13.

Many factors must be taken into account in deciding where in a state or region a new college should be located. Among the more important ones are the following:

1. *The potential need for a new college.*

The indices of need have already been considered. In the case of junior colleges, a minimum enrollment of 400 is suggested as a basis for justifying a new institution.[20] Since practically all junior college students come from the immediate area, future enrollments can be estimated with considerable accuracy. The same is not true of new senior colleges. The minimum enrollment for efficient operation of a senior college is generally considered to be 1,000 but some state master plans set a much higher minimum. The Master Plan for Higher Education in California, for example, specifies a minimum of 5,000 in metropolitan areas and of 3,000 outside of metropolitan centers. Whereas junior colleges are designed to provide educational opportunities to the youth of a definitely delimited area, senior colleges generally serve larger areas and sometimes a more highly selected student clientele. Some senior colleges serve largely a constituency in a metropolitan center or a region of a state. In fact, most senior colleges draw a majority of their students from a radius of not more than 200 miles. There are some, however, that are national rather than local or regional because their prestige enables them to select students from both a national and an international clientele, because they serve a special constituency, or because they offer unusual types of programs. The need for a senior college must, therefore, be determined by the need of a total constituency — state-wide, and regional or national — in the case of public colleges; church-wide or regional and national in the case of private colleges. This wider distribution of potential students increases the difficulty of establishing a locus of greatest need.

Both wisdom and experience dictate that new senior colleges should be located in close proximity to established or emerging metropolitan centers. The advantages of such a location are ready access to diverse cultural resources, opportunities for part-time employment, easy access by highways and public transportation, and possibilities of off-campus living accommodations. Over the years some colleges in smaller isolated communities have found it advantageous to move to larger centers of population. Exceptions to this principle are found among recently established new

---

[20]A. J. Brumbaugh, *Guidelines for the Establishment of Community Junior Colleges* (Atlanta, Georgia: Southern Regional Education Board, 1963), p. 9.

private senior colleges. Without questioning the wisdom of their location it should be observed that outstanding advantages must be identified to counterbalance ready access to a sizable center of population.

The projected maximum size of the new college also has an important bearing on location. If the college is conceived to have a maximum enrollment of 1,000, 1,500, or 2,000 students attracted from a broad geographical area by the distinctiveness of its program, the attractiveness of its setting may be more important than its proximity to a metropolitan center. Even in such a concept of a new college, the cultural advantages of a metropolitan center should not be overlooked.

The location of other colleges in the area — junior and senior, public and private — must be taken into account. The location of a number of community junior colleges in an area might argue strongly for an upper level senior college (junior, senior years and possibly graduate work leading to the master's degree) to provide advanced education for students who should continue beyond the junior college. Conversely, the location of one or more private senior colleges in an area may argue against the establishment of another senior college in the same area. This argument should not be carried to the point at which the educational interests of an appreciable number of youth are unprovided for. Even though private colleges are available, an appraisal of the situation will require an assessment of the capacities of the existing institutions, the costs involved in attending them, the degree of selective admission exercised, and the appropriateness of the programs to the educational needs of the youth. Where the capacity of existing private colleges in the area is adequate to provide for potential demand and programs are appropriate, consideration may be given to some type of contractual arrangement between the state or municipality and the private colleges for educational services. In some situations, this will be impracticable because it involves the use of public funds to support private institutions and because private institutions resist the implications of creeping public control.

The issue of the use of public funds to support private institutions can be met by making available scholarship aid to students that will enable them to attend the private colleges. This may still be a more economical way of fully utilizing available facilities and of providing appropriate opportunities than to establish another college in the area.

2. *Economic considerations.*

The availability of land and the cost of its acquisition are

54

important in the determination of the location of a new college. The location of a college in a community brings both cultural and economic benefits. Not only is the college an incentive to raise the educational level of the community and a source of ideas for community improvement, but it also has a direct impact on the economy of the community. It is quite understandable, therefore, that communities should vie with one another to attract a new college. Generally, communities attach enough value to having a college to make a site available without cost and sometimes to add other financial inducements either in pledges of cash support or in various kinds of services — utilities, transportation, and tax exemptions.

These inducements may complicate the problem of finding a suitable location, both because communities become competitive in their offers and because those responsible for making the decision may be influenced unduly by what appears to be a marked immediate economic advantage.

The location of a new college is a long-term proposition. It would be much wiser for an extra million or two million dollars to be spent to acquire the right location than for the new institution to live its entire life under the handicap of a wrong decision.

3. *Geographic-geological considerations.*

Access to a new college is another factor in deciding on a location. Highways and airlines are particularly important. If it is anticipated that the college will serve a commuting as well as a residential clientele, access by major highways becomes a matter of primary importance. Even students who will live on the campus will drive or be driven to the institution or they will rely on air transportation.

If the college is to be located within easy reach of the cultural advantages of a metropolitan center, access by highway and by public transportation to the cultural resources must be considered.

The topographical characteristics of the site — whether it is mountainous or flat, whether it is intersected by water courses, and whether adequate drainage seems to be provided by the natural lay of the land — must be taken into account. Important as these factors are, the sub-surface soil of the area may be even more important. Large underground caverns or sink holes, soft rock or water-laden loam may make the construction of firm foundations for buildings very costly. Deep borings to determine the nature of the sub-surface structure is an indispensable step in site selection.

A further factor to be taken into account is the potential economic development of the area. Industrial growth is commonly associated with metropolitan development. The nature of the industries and the direction in which they expand make a great difference in determining the location of a new college. Some industries are so artistically housed and landscaped that they are an asset to a community. Others, like steel industries, cement plants, strip mining, and oil refineries by their very nature are unsightly and incompatible with a college environment.

Campus Planning

The preceding section has presented some of the broader issues affecting the selection of a location for a new senior college. Many more specific issues about the use of the site that is selected and plans for the buildings that will be constructed remain to be considered.

The size of the campus is the first consideration. The United States Office of Education reports that for 31 new private liberal arts colleges that opened between 1961 and 1965, the range in campus size was from 22 to 800 acres with a mean of 254 acres. For 7 public liberal arts colleges the mean was 437 acres. Twenty-two acres may be a large block of land if it is located in the heart of a metropolitan area; 800 acres may not be unusual if it is located in an open area as, for example, an airbase that has become surplus government property or a tract that is donated by a philanthropist as part of a community development project. The minimum land requirement will depend on the anticipated size of the institution and on the plan for land utilization. Ordinarily, at least 250 acres, the approximate mean for 31 private colleges, would seem to be the desirable minimum as a setting for a college enrolling about 1,000 students.

As larger enrollments are envisaged, the expanse of the campus should be increased. It is not uncommon for a new college that will ultimately enroll 10,000 or more students to acquire a site of at least 1,000 acres, but availability, planned land use, and location will be large determining factors.

The first step in the development of the physical setting and facilities for a new college, once the site has been selected, is to design a plan for the most effective use of the available land. So many new colleges have been established in recent years that there is a wealth of experience from which can be derived suggestions of constructive ideas and of errors. There is also an extensive body of literature that summarizes planning procedures and presents imaginative ideas. Because of the availability of these experiences and materials, consideration is given here only to certain factors — some quite obvious — that must be taken into account in designing an overall plan for land utilization. Among those to be kept in mind are the following:

1. *The size of the site.*

As has already been noted, the land area of liberal arts college campuses typically is about 250 acres. If a new college is to be located either in the heart of a metropolitan area, or in its suburbs, as for example the Chicago branch of the University of Illinois or the new protestant college in the suburbs of Honolulu, available land may be highly restricted — 46 acres with possibility of expansion to 105 acres in Chicago, 100 acres in Honolulu. On the other hand, a new college may be located within commuting distance of a metropolitan center, yet be located in wide open spaces where large tracts become available — 1200 acres for Florida Atlantic University; almost 1800 acres for the University of South Florida. Or if the college is to be completely residential, removed from a large center of population, it may have 2,000 acres or more, as was true of Principia College when it moved to a new site some years ago. There is no standard index of size of a site in relation to the size of institution, but the land available is an important controlling factor in planning.

2. *Topography is also a controlling condition in planning land use.*

An area of 500 or 1,000 acres of perfectly flat terrain without trees presents a contrast to a tract of equal size that is hilly and wooded. If the level tract is interlaced with the concrete runways of a former airbase, some of which may be used as parking areas, the design for land utilization will have to be quite different from the design for the use of an equally level tract that has been artificially created in part by a fill on a waterfront. This may seem like laboring the obvious, but it is justified by the apparent failure in some instances to consider natural contour in selecting a site or to capitalize on natural assets once it has been selected. On the other hand, there are striking examples of planning that have fully exploited natural assets.

3. *A third factor in planning land utilization is safety.*

Traffic hazards must be kept at a minimum by providing access roads that lead into parking areas without dangerous intersections.

The actual or contemplated location of limited access highways and location of highway interchanges may influence the location of access roads to the campus, perimeter roads on the campus, and the location of parking areas. Also, access roads must be located so that they do not cross paths of heavy pedestrian traffic. Where a public highway intersects a college site in such a way that students must cross the highway, safety requires that overhead or underground passageways be built. In such a situation, legal arrangements for the construction of the passageways should be made with public authorities when the land is acquired.

4. *Of no small importance are such matters as availability of utilities — light, gas, water, fire protection, and sewage disposal.*

Not only the availability of these services but their access to the site, particularly for fire protection and sewage disposal, may have an important bearing on plans for land utilization.

With these and other special considerations in mind, a comprehensive design of the entire campus must be drawn. This is an assignment for a specialist in campus planning in collaboration with the administration and with contracting architects. The outcome of this collaboration will be the designation of areas or zones for discrete institutional functions and services. Because a number of excellent comprehensive treatises on campus planning are available, there is no point in going into details here.* It is appropriate, however, to consider basic concepts and guiding principles that are involved in making an overall design. A pertinent general observation is expressed in the following statement:

> Accepting all these as planning problems, it is evident that physical plans must be both general and specific; they must be concerned with immediate requirements as well as long-range considerations; they must cover the campus and environs as well as specific building sites; and they must implement today's educational goals while at the same time encourage, if they can, but not hinder, new objectives. Plans as an instrument by which the campus administration can make good decisions should reflect the institution's point of view of land-use development, incorporate the widest range of opinions as to how the institution should grow but restrict such opinions as to reasonable alternatives . . . . Plans must be practical and plans must be imaginative.[21]

Related functions or services should be located in a designated

---

*Several references are included in the bibliography of this brochure.
[21]Richard C. Dober, *Campus Planning* (New York: Reinhold Publishing Corporation, 1963), p. 45.

area. An overall campus design should include the following specific provisions:

1. *Since the most important functions are instruction and related research, these should constitute the focus of the campus design.*

The size of the area thus designated will be governed by the ultimate size of the enrollment, by the scope of the educational program and by the methods of teaching that will be used. Two practical considerations to be kept in mind are: allow ample space for expansion and incorporate a high degree of flexibility. Many a time an institution is caught short on ground space because it was originally conceived in terms of a limited registration, but under new conditions and pressures it has to abandon its original concept. Likewise, a college that sets out as a single purpose liberal arts institution may expand the scope of its program to conform to new and broader purposes. The area allocated to academic facilities will also be determined by the type of facilities to be built. Whether they are to be highrise structures or low, widespread buildings will be an important controlling factor.

A word of warning is in order at this point. Some institutions, either because of the lay of the land or because of poor planning, have classroom buildings, the library, and the laboratories so widely separated that students have difficulty in getting from one to the other within a reasonable time limit. Morever, if they have to depend on their own automobiles to get from one part of the campus to another, both parking problems and traffic hazards are created.

2. *Another functional area should be designated for residences.*

Here again, not only the number of students to be accommodated, but also the student mix — male, female; graduate, undergraduate; married, single — and the type of housing — highrise or low — will affect the size of the land area required. Obviously, allowance must be made for children's playgrounds and recreation if married students are housed on the campus.

There should also be easy access from residences to recreation facilities — tennis courts, swimming pool, golf course, athletic fields and gymnasium without intruding on the areas of academic activities.

A question arises about the provision of faculty housing on the campus. If it is to be provided, should it be on a separate site or should it be included in the campus residential area?

3. *Physical education, recreation, and sports constitute a group of related activities that should be located in an area removed from the center of academic activities, but, as already suggested, within easy access of the residence centers.*

The land area required obviously will depend on the nature and scope of the recreation and sports program. If such activities as golf and equitation are to be provided, large areas must be designated for these activities; if these are not involved, the land area can be limited accordingly.

4. *There must also be areas designated for shops, storage, and other kinds of service facilities.*

These illustrations suffice to support the idea that related activities and functions should be identified with designated land areas. Assuming that educational facilities are centrally located and other functions and services radiate toward the periphery, a typical campus design might be as shown in Figure 2.

Planning Physical Facilities

Once a general design for land use has been drawn, the next important step is to plan the physical facilities that will constitute the base of operations for the new college. A visit to college and university campuses throughout the nation with a view to getting ideas of architectural structure and style would be quite as confusing as enlightening. It would identify the historic Gothic-Monastic, stately and impressive but out of date; the Georgian, which in its purest form, gave character to the campus of the College of William and Mary and in modified, if not corrupted, form is represented by "old Main" on many a campus. The most distressing effect of such a tour will be the hodge-podge of buildings on many campuses that show no consistent planning, but reflect eras of architects and administrators who left their legacy of distinctive but unharmonious building design. But these unharmonious collections of college buildings on a campus need not continue if a rational plan is established and if the skills of building designers are aptly applied. Until the last quarter century, college architecture was largely historically oriented. Now, since there have emerged strikingly new modernistic functional buildings, plans point to the future instead of to the past.

Despite the lack of architectural consistency and harmony on many campuses, an excursion among the campuses of the nation, old and new, may suggest guiding principles and concepts that

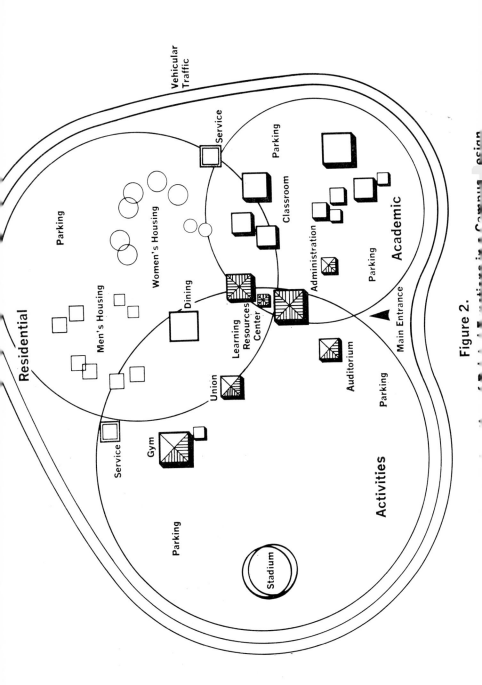

Figure 2.

61

will lead to satisfying achievements. It isn't necessary, in fact, for every administrator, architect, and campus planner to make such a tour for there is a considerable body of published information that will give in condensed form the benefits of numerous observations. Among those that will be found particularly valuable are Dober, *Campus Planning;* Rork and Robbins, *Case Book on Campus Planning and Institutional Development,* U. S. Office of Education; Jamrich, *To Build or Not to Build,* Educational Facilities Laboratory; Robbins and Bokelman, *College and University Facilities Survey,* U. S. Office of Education.

Some of the most important concepts and guiding principles derived from these sources and from personal observation follow:

1. *Form should serve rather than control function.*

Until recently, buildings were designed according to standard architectural patterns and functions were assigned to or crammed into space limits. Unfortunately, this continues to be true too often, especially where state building authorities or architectural firms with little experience in planning college buildings design facilities with little or no participation in planning by the institutional administration and faculty. But now it is increasingly recognized that form should serve function.

Both the faculty and the administration should have an important role in defining the objectives of the institution and the pattern of the curriculum to serve those objectives. Functions thus derived can be classified as central to the college program and, therefore, to be centrally located, or as ancillary and, therefore, to be located adjacent to the central functions. Central functions will include provisions for reading and study activities located in the library, and related learning facilities and resources; instruction requiring classrooms, laboratories, studios, lecture rooms, conference rooms, and teaching auditorium; and administrative and management functions. Among the ancillary functions are food services; student recreation and informal social activities of the type usually found in a student union building; health and recreational activities; student housing; cultural events — lectures, recitals, exhibits — for both the campus and the public; recreational and sports events open to the public; ample parking spaces for students and for guests, on public occasions; facilities and services — power, water, building and equipment maintenance — essential to the efficient operation of the college plant.

Research by faculty and students is a somewhat specialized function that must be considered in college planning. It is mentioned specifically because the opportunity to do independent research is frequently given as a reason why faculty members prefer a university appointment over one in a liberal arts college. In planning space distribution and utilization, therefore, it is wise to provide small faculty research laboratories.

There is also a growing emphasis on research by students. Science fairs in high schools and the search for science talent lend impetus to the experimental interests of students. To enable experimentally minded students to continue their research from he time they enter college would seem to be not only justified but imperative. Because student experiments often require private facilities both for continuity and accuracy, student research laboratories should be incorporated into space design. These, too, should be included in the space plan.

Policies will differ from one college to another on some of these functions. For example, generally the provision for the public to participate in cultural and recreational events is accepted as a desirable campus function; yet one institution reported that in drafting a master plan for its campus, "It was determined that the master plan should be designed entirely for the students, faculty, and staff of the institution, not for the general public. Toward this end every building and other facility on the campus fronted on an interior area and turned its back to the surrounding streets and neighborhoods. The interior area, or 'quad' became the functional center of the entire campus."

Concerning the location of buildings in the same institution, strict attention was paid to the function of each building.

> Thus the gymnasium was located as near as possible to the playing field. The large building housing the little theatre and auditorium was moved from its first site (determined earlier by the state division of architecture) to another corner of the campus; the first site was adjacent to a main north-south highway where parking would always be limited; the new site selected was adjacent to a parking area that is yet available and many blocks of peripheral side-street parking. The cafeteria was placed directly adjacent to the future student union building which is yet to be financed. The only time the principle of function was somewhat modified was when the library was placed at one side of the central area; from the standpoint of function, it should have been built in the center of the "quad," but it was decided that moving it to the side would add to the beauty of the campus and detract but slightly from its efficient function.[22]

---

[22]*Casebook on Campus Planning and Institutional Development. op. cit.*, p. 82.

63

2. Economy and efficiency.

Both economy and efficiency are important interrelated considerations in planning new college buildings. One of the great extravagances in many existing institutions is poor space utilization. Classrooms are used only a small percentage of the hours per week that they are available and the seating capacity far exceeds the size of classes assigned to them. A study of space utilization in 53 colleges showed that the percentage of possible use of classrooms based on a 44-hour week ranged from a low of 21 to a high of 61; for teaching laboratories the corresponding figures were 10 percent low and 44 percent high. One important factor influencing classroom utilization is the tendency to concentrate the schedule of classes in certain preferred hours of the day and on certain days of the week.

Equally wasteful is low utilization of student stations in classrooms. Data on student station use in a 44-hour week ranged from a low of 10 to a high of 39. For teaching laboratories the range is even greater from a low of six percent to a high of 50 percent. These data are cited merely to reinforce the fact that economy in space use will be governed by a number of considerations. One of the most important is the size of enrollment in relation to the number of fields of specialization; a limited enrollment in a college offering a large number of majors will almost inevitably result in a disproportionate number of small classes. Studies show that the lowest percentage of space use is found in colleges that have the highest percentage of classes enrolling fewer than 10 students. Both the organization of the curriculum and the size of enrollment must, therefore, be taken into account.

Another consideration is the plan of instruction that is envisaged. If the emphasis is to be placed on independent study, honors courses, and seminars, the size and kind of instructional space that will be required will be quite different than if the plan contemplates large lecture groups supplemented by discussion groups. Current trends suggest that both the shortage of college teachers and the use of new methods and media of instruction will lead to a marked increase in the number of students per faculty member. The ratio of 20 students per faculty member suggested by the late Beardsley Ruml in his *Memo to a College Trustee* may be realized sooner than the author anticipated.

In the interest of both economy and efficiency, multiple use may be made of some space. Two illustrations will suffice. Corridors and enclosed connecting walks between buildings can be used for various kinds of displays — student art, original or reproductions of works of famous artists, science models, geological specimens, Americana, portraits of statesmen, actors, authors, artists, musicians — the possibilities become exciting. Also, studios and laboratories may serve multiple purposes. A group of scientists and mathematicians who constituted a task force for planning the science facilities of a new institution recommended that "instruction in the sciences and mathematics be organized and administered as a single program utilizing common facilities wherever possible."

Facilities planned to serve clearly defined functions economically and efficiently will be work places rather than replicas of historical and traditional patterns.

3. Unity.

Unity, an important characteristic of new college facilities, has several different implications. First, it implies an interrelatedness, a congruity among buildings designed to serve various educational functions. This sense of unity may derive from consistency in style; the orderly arrangement of buildings from a central focus to a peripheral location; provisions of artistically designed walkways sheltered or enclosed to connect buildings, and landscape design.

Second, unity is, or should be, a cherished characteristic of human relationships on a campus. Various conditions within the college that promote separateness of groups are the segmentation of the program and consequently of the faculty into divisions or colleges, each having its own locus of operation; the division of the student body into residential and commuting, fraternity and non-fraternity; or favored athletic groups. Faculty members make the faculty club their meeting place; students meet in the student union, the dining hall, the snack bar, and in common rooms in their residences. Not all of these tendencies to separateness and isolation are found on every campus. Nor are they as common in the small colleges as they are in the larger ones, but they do occur with sufficient frequency to merit consideration in planning new college facilities. To find countervailing factors is a challenge to the imagination of the planner.

Among the suggestions that have been made or tried are these: (1) establish a learning resources center as a focus of the intellectual life of the campus. In this center would be located the library, language and programmed learning laboratories, study booths equipped with slide projectors and dialing systems for tape recordings; projection rooms for running or re-running video tapes; a collection of art slides and the provision of projectors for their use; a collection of records in listening rooms; testing and counseling facilities; student-faculty conference rooms, and other learning resources. (2) Provide study rooms for commuting students which would be a counterpart of the dormitories for residential students. These should be built on the same style and plan as residential dormitories with common entrances, common lounges, and common residential heads. It is believed that some of the sharp lines between commuting and resident students can thus be erased.

It has been proposed in this connection that were some faculty members to have offices in these residential units, the ties between students and faculty might be strengthened. While there may be considerable doubt as to the feasibility of this arrangement because faculty members resist having offices detached from the locus of their academic activities, it is altogether feasible to hold faculty-student "bull-sessions" in the common rooms of student residences. (3) Provide all-campus cultural events that will bring together students and faculty from various disciplines with opportunities for students to meet visiting artists. The artist in residence — an extension of this idea — is highly acclaimed by students. (4) Provide laboratories for undirected student expression and experimentation in the arts; opportunities for students to dabble in various media of art, not only afford a type of recreation, sometimes therapeutic, but also may disclose special artistic talent. Provisions for periodic exhibits of selected productions provide an incentive to experimentation and a focus of student interest.

Related to this element of unity, the plan for a new church-related college contains this significant statement:

> The plan should both symbolize and promote the element of community which will be fundamental to every aspect of the college's life. Whether this Christian symbolism can be achieved by building the college around a center . . . or by placing the chapel at the apex of a V-shaped campus is not important so long as some adequately symbolic concept is used as a guide.[23]

No illustrations are needed to emphasize two further points. First, that the unifying factors on a campus must be identified and incorporated into the campus plans; second, that appropriate facilities for essential unifying functions must be included in the plant design.

---

[23]Dober, *op. cit.*, p. 201.

4. Flexibility.

An essential characteristic of new physical facilities is flexibility. Flexibility relates to provision for modification or expansion in the design of buildings. Unless facilities are constructed initially for the maximum anticipated enrollment, provisions for their expansion must be included both in the campus plan and in the building designs. For example, in a new college where a learning resources center is the focus of the educational plant, some phases of the activities in the center may expand beyond initial expectations. Others may fall short of anticipated use. Space devoted to these variable functions should be readily convertible according to demand.

Changes in curriculum and in methods of teaching are to be expected unless a new college quickly becomes static and inflexible. These, too, will require modifications of classrooms and lecture halls in size and arrangement and possibly new kinds of fixtures and equipment.

Flexibility has special relevance to student housing and food service. If, as has already been suggested, a center to provide private study rooms for commuting students is incorporated in the student housing complex, the interior plan should be such that it can be readily converted to the use of residential students should that become desirable or necessary. Also, the ratio of male to female students may vary as much as 15 percent from one year to the next. Here again, flexibility demands that residential units be so located and constructed that they can accommodate these variations in enrollments.

Architects and building planners will provide for flexibility by appropriate location of weight-bearing walls; by installation of movable partitions; by strategic location of windows; and by proper location of water and sewer pipes and utility conduits.

The most important characteristic of our day is change. If higher education is to keep pace with this phenomenon it, too, must be susceptible to change, sometimes radical change. Flexibility is the element of physical facilities that accommodates rather than inhibits change.

5. Harmony.

Harmony is the effect achieved by the distinctive design of buildings and of the landscape that provides their setting. Under the impact of rapid expansion and enforced economies, college architectural style as expressed in the collegiate gothic and the Georgian architecture that have given character and identity to some campuses, has been sacrificed to utility. Some campuses that were once models of harmony have been invaded by modern designs. The total effect is not always unpleasant, but in too many instances, it jars aesthetic sensitivities. Dober observes that "the visual chaos now apparent on many heterogeneous campuses need not continue if a rational structure is established through planning and if the skills of the designer are used to reinforce structure."[24]

A new college starting from scratch is free from predetermined style and, therefore, can set its own standards of harmony. In doing so, however, several important facts should be kept in mind.

First, the decades since World War II have been a period of great inventiveness in architecture. A variety of new styles has appeared and still more may be anticipated. While these largely supersede the conventional historic gothic and Georgian, there are as yet no new styles that are as well established as were the historic styles when they were approved. In deciding on an architectural style, it is of prime importance to think in long-range terms and to apply a criterion of continuing modernity. In Dober's words, "This year's fashion may be next year's failure."

The new college campus is not the place to experiment with the exotic. Such experiments may be appropriate for world's fair buildings, airports, motels, or artists' colonies, but not for a new college. Nor should an architectural style be adopted, merely because it bears the name of a distinguished architect, though it may bear testimony to his artistry.

Second, style is to some extent a product of homogenuity with environment. Building materials indigenous to one area, for example, Indiana limestone or Georgian marble, are quite well adapted to the areas in which they are found. In areas having a semi-tropical climate as, for example, the Gulf states, the materials that are in harmony with the climate and cultural atmosphere of the area should be used. In other words, in some regions the style of architecture may express protection against hostile natural elements, in others it may capitalize on hospitable elements. Harmony results from architecture that blends with the landscape unified by ingeniously planned walks, gardens, and vistas.

---

[24]Dober, *op. cit.*, p. 220.

CHAPTER 3

FINANCING A NEW COLLEGE

The accurate projection of the costs of a new college is basic to the establishment of a new institution. Gross errors of estimation may in fact handicap a college for many years. Making these estimates is, however, a complicated procedure because of the many factors that must be taken into account.

Financial patterns for the operating budget and for capital construction are so fundamentally different that they will be considered separately. For each, attention will be given to methods for estimating needs and also to sources of financial support. Before discussing them, however, certain general considerations which are relevant to all aspects of finance will be noted.

Financial projections must be based upon a knowledge of the projected program of the new institution. Among the important program variables which will affect projections are the following:

1. The stages in which the college will begin operation. Will only freshmen be admitted during the first year, or will a full program be offered? Will the physical facilities be built sequentially over a period of years, or will the plant be fully completed at the time of initial occupancy?

2. The initial and ultimate enrollment, and the student "mix" in that enrollment. What will be the proportion of freshmen, sophomores, juniors, and seniors? What proportions will be men and women, married and single, residential and commuting?

3. The type of curriculum to be offered, and the relative emphasis to be placed upon various parts of the curriculum. What proportion of the enrollment will be in the sciences, humanities, and social sciences? What special professional or occupational programs are planned? What do these curricular emphases imply in terms of requirements for staff, library, equipment and physical facilities?

69

4. Instructional methods to be employed. What degree of emphasis will be placed upon the use of large classes, programmed learning, televised instruction, independent study, and other innovations which will have implications for the type of staff, equipment, and physical facilities that will be needed?

5. The proposed student-faculty ratio. What implications will this have for salaries, office space, and research laboratories?

6. The counseling program. How is the need for staff and office space affected by the type and extent of counseling that is planned?

7. Resident student arrangements. What proportion of the student body is to be residential, and what should be the relationship of the residential space to the educational program and facilities?

8. The nature and scope of physical education and sports activities.

These and other program factors will have a major influence on both the operating costs and the cost of physical facilities.

ESTIMATING OPERATING COSTS

Among the conditions that affect operating costs are the purposes of the college and the scope and depth of the programs designed to achieve those purposes. It must be borne in mind that the more comprehensive the purposes of a new college are, the broader and more varied will be the program required to achieve them.

The projected size of the student body has a bearing on estimated costs in several respects. If an educational program of considerable scope is offered, with a number of fields of specialization, the enrollment should be of sufficient size to avoid an excessive number of small classes. There is convincing evidence that the percent of classes having enrollments of ten or less tends to be comparatively higher in colleges with small total enrollments, and that the average cost per student credit hour is also high at small colleges.

An enrollment of approximately 1,000 students is considered to be the minimal size at which a liberal arts college can operate at a level of economic efficiency. Earl J. McGrath suggests that a small institution which wishes to improve its financial position can do so (1) by raising its enrollment to 1,200 to 1,500 students. (2) by keeping the number of low-enrollment advanced courses which are offered as near as possible to the number required for a major and (3) by developing a general education program with quite large classes.[1]

Table 2—Selected Factors Related to the Cost of Instruction in 13 Liberal Arts Colleges

Enrollment	Average Cost Per Student Credit Hour	Average Class Size	Per Cent Of Classes Under 11
620	$16.34	14.70	44.11
734	15.80	14.97	42.42
785	9.39	23.63	21.43
844	14.25	15.19	39.64
910	15.37	18.63	27.48
938	17.79	17.71	33.89
1,015	13.77	16.81	35.04
1,025	14.44	18.44	29.64
1,155	7.86	23.00	22.00
1,145	12.80	19.40	28.38
1,164	9.04	21.75	21.70
1,228	14.28	19.49	24.66
1,591	10.49	20.98	17.44

Source: Adapted from Table IV, "Comparative Figures for 13 Colleges of Liberal Arts Concerning Various Factors Related to the Cost of Instruction," Earl J. McGrath, *Memo To A College Faculty Member* (New York: Teachers College, Columbia University, 1961), p. 29.

Table 2, based on work done by McGrath, summarizes the relationship of several functions to the cost per student credit hour in 13 liberal arts colleges. The colleges are arranged by size of enrollment. The table clearly reveals the general relationship between size and cost. As enrollment grows larger, there is a tendency for the average cost per student credit hour to *decrease,* for the percentage of classes with fewer than 11 students to *decrease,* and for the average size of classes to *increase.* The exceptions to this generalization should be noted, however. Some colleges in the group do not fit the generalization because they have chosen, consciously to have an unusually high or low (1) number of course offerings, (2) average class size or (3) average faculty salary.

[1]Earl J. McGrath, *Memo to a College Faculty Member* (New York: Bureau of Publications, Teachers College, Columbia University, 1961), p. 29.

With proper control of the proliferation of courses, with a corresponding limitation of the number of small classes, and with the maintenance of a defensible number of large classes, higher faculty salaries and fringe benefits can be paid without inflating instructional costs per student credit hour. Not only McGrath's investigations, but also the work done by Ruml and Morrison support this point of view.[2] In their discussion Ruml and Morrison present several "Models of the Possible," which suggest for liberal arts colleges of various sizes, combinations of courses and plans of instruction that will afford faculty salaries at a level that will "bring high talent into faculties." While the data they use for illustrative purposes may have to be revised, the principles illustrated are highly relevant to planning and operating a budget for a new liberal arts college.

By way of illustration, the following examples taken from the "Models of the Possible,"[3] show two suggested combinations of courses for a college of 1,200 students and a possible salary distribution based on tuition income at $800 per student.

First Alternate Possible Combination of Courses for a 1,200 Student College
(Ruml-Morrison)

8	large lecture courses averaging 300 students	2400	course registrations
52	lecture-discussion courses averaging 75 students	3900	course registrations
300	seminar-tutorial courses averaging 11 students	3300	course registrations
360	courses or sections	9600	course registrations

Second Alternate Possible Combination of Courses for a 1,200 Student College
(Ruml-Morrison)

20	large lecture courses averaging 120 students	2400	course registrations
40	lecture-discussion courses averaging 60 students	2400	course registrations
300	seminar-tutorial courses averaging 16 students	4800	course registrations
360	courses or sections	9600	course registrations

---

[2]Beardsley Ruml and Donald H. Morrison, *Memo to a College Trustee* (New York: McGraw-Hill Book Company, Inc., 1959).

[3]*Ibid.*, p. 38.

Possible Salary Distribution for a College with 1,200 Students
and 60 Faculty Members
(Ruml-Morrison)

Total faculty compensation		$960,000
Less 15% for retirement and insurance		
benefits and 10% for sabbatical-leave reserve . .		240,000
Balance available for salary payments		$720,000

Distribution of faculty salaries

10 averaging	$ 7,500	. . . .	$ 75,000
15 "	10,000	. . . .	150,000
15 "	12,000	. . . .	180,000
10 "	15,000	. . . .	150,000
10 "	16,500	. . . .	165,000
60 averaging	$12,000		$720,000

Another item in the operating budget that varies with the size of the institution is general administration and general expense. General administration costs tend to be higher in colleges of small enrollment because the size of administrative staff and of general expense cannot be reduced below a certain minimum. Data illustrating this fact are presented in a report of 1963-64 current fund expenditures in Southern institutions published by the Commission on Colleges and Universities of the Southern Association of Colleges and Schools.[4] Table 3, adapted from that report, summarizes data from a total of 440 institutions.

The four expenditure categories listed in this table represent the major educational and general budget accounts that should be considered in estimating operating costs. Once again it is apparent that the cost *per student* decreases as the enrollment increases. It also is apparent that the *percentage* of total expenditures which has to be spent for administration declines, allowing a larger percentage to be spent for instruction.

Extension and public services, which are not included, are important on some campuses. The magnitude of the extension and public services planned for a new college should be clearly defined. It will include adult education courses, public lectures, radio and television lectures, institutes and workshops, and community services. Initially these activities may not be expensive; nevertheless, an estimated cost must be included in a projected operating budget.

---

[4] Gustave Ernest Metz, *Current Fund Expenditures* (Atlanta, Georgia: Southern Association of Colleges and Schools, 1964), p. 33.

Table 3—Four Basic Educational and General Expenditures
Medians in Dollars Per Student, and Percent of Total Educational and General Expenditures, 1963-1954.

Institutions by Highest Level of Offerings with Subgroups by Enrollments	Medians in Dollars Spent per Student					Medians in Percent of Total Educational and General Expenditures Spent for Each Item				
	Gen. Adm. and Gen. Exp.a	Instr. and Dept. Researchb	Libraries	Oper. and Maint.c	Totald	Gen. Adm. and Gen. Exp.a	Instr. and Dept. Researchb	Libraries	Oper. and Maint.c	Totald
Bachelor's Level:										
0-499........	310	550	58	147	1065	27	53	5.5	13	98.5
500-999........	274	500	56	146	976	27	51	5.4	14	97.4
1000 & Over.....	193	462	44	126	825	21	56	5.5	15	97.5
Master's Level:										
0- 999........	302	645	63	148	1158	25	53	5.1	13	96.1
1000-2499........	176	545	50	142	913	20	55	5.6	15	95.6
2500 & Over.....	113	460	39	110	722	15	62	4.7	14	95.7

aGeneral administration and general expense
bInstruction and departmental research
cOperation and maintenance of the physical plant
dTotal of the costs accounted for by these four categories

Source: Adapted from Table 13, "Four Basic Educational and General Expenditures—Administration and General Expense, Instruction and Departmental Research, Library, and Operation and Maintenance of the Physical Plant," Gustave Ernest Metz, *Current Fund Expenditures* (Atlanta: Southern Association of Colleges and Schools, 1964), p. 33.

The expenditure categories listed also excluded "auxiliary enterprises" such as dormitories and dining halls. At most colleges these are assumed to be either self-supporting or income producing. They need be considered in estimating operating costs only insofar as they involve expenditures beyond income produced. Based on 1963-64 data of the Southern Association, if a new four-year college of 1,000 students were being established in the South, the estimated basic operating cost would be as follows:

Gen. Adm. and Gen. Exp.
(1,000 Students x $193 per student) $193,000
Instr. and Dept. Research
(1,000 Students x $462 per student) 462,000
Libraries (1,000 Students x $44 per student) . . 44,000
Oper. and Maint.
(1,000 Student x $126 per student) 126,000
Other Operating Costs
(2.5% according to data in Table 2) 21,150

Total $846,150

The actual experience of recently established senior colleges suggests that this estimate is low.

Another approach is to compute the number of faculty personnel required, using current national data, then to determine instructional costs by applying the most recent salary figures, and then to estimate total costs by the use of relevant percentages. In 1961-62 the national and Southern student-faculty ratio was 17:1.[5] On the basis of this ratio, a faculty of 53 would be needed for 1,000 students.

Nationally the median salary for faculty members of all ranks in state colleges in 1965-66 was $8,750; in private colleges enrolling 1,000 or more it was $8,214.[6] Using the larger of these medians, the faculty salary costs at a college of 1,000 students would be $463,750. Faculty salary costs represent approximately 80% of the "instruction and departmental research" costs of most colleges, so that the total instructional cost would be in the neighborhood of $580,000. Various studies have shown that in a college enrolling 1,000 or more students the amount spent for instruction and departmental research is approximately 50 percent of the

---

[5]E. F. Schietinger, *Fact Book on Higher Education in the South, 1965* (Atlanta, Georgia: Southern Regional Education Board, 1965), p. 46.

[6]*Salaries in Higher Education 1965-66* (Washington, D. C.: Research Division, National Education Association, 1966), p. 11.

total educational and general expenditures. Applying this figure to estimated instructional costs of $580,000, the total educational and general expenditures would be $1,160,000.

It would probably be more realistic to use the salary level at the third quartile, which for institutions of 1,000 students was $10,301 in state colleges and $9,748 in private colleges. Computed on the higher of these two figures, total salaries for 53 faculty members would be $545,953 and the total educational and general expenditures would be $1,364,825.

The two methods outlined above for estimating educational and general costs indicate that these costs would range from $846,000 to $1,364,000. Taking into account the increase of salary costs at the rate of approximately five percent annually and allowing for items not included in the foregoing analysis, an annual operating budget of $1,000,000 to $1,500,000 might be regarded as conservative.

Evidence substantiating these estimates may be derived from

Table 4—Per-Student Operating Expenditures at New Four-Year Colleges, Mid-1960's

Full-time Equivalent Enrollment	Expenditure Per Full-time Equivalent Student	Total Operating Expenditures
285	$1,193	$ 339,965
300	2,770	829,000
500	1,996	997,822
530	2,290	1,213,696
541	1,260	681,785
581	875	508,612
600	1,644[a]	986,862[a]
772	1,499	1,572,366
795	865	687,746
886	1,287	1,139,962
3,706	677	2,510,141

a "Operating Expenditures" includes student aid at this institution.

The institutions included are:
Eisenhower College (New York)
Florida Presbyterian College
Grand Valley State College (Michigan)
Houston Baptist College (Texas)
Kentucky Southern College
Methodist College (North Carolina)
Mobile College (Alabama)
North Carolina Wesleyan College
Oklahoma Christian College
St. Andrew's Presbyterian College (North Carolina)
Southern Colorado State College

the actual operating budgets of several recently established senior colleges. The data in Table 4 were provided by eleven new colleges. It is worth noting that most of these institutions are too new for the normal relationship of enrollment to per-student costs to have become apparent. In its early years an institution usually cannot operate at optimum cost levels.

SOURCES OF SUPPORT FOR OPERATING COSTS

Once estimates have been made of operating costs, consideration must be given to a realistic appraisal of possible sources of financial support. The sources of financial support utilized by already established liberal arts colleges may afford important leads. The percentage of income derived from various sources by public and private liberal arts colleges in 1959-60 is shown in Table 5.

The data show that the sources of finance for public and private institutions are almost completely different. In 1959-60 public liberal arts colleges derived 80.2 percent of their support

Table 5—Percent of Income for Educational and General Purposes
(except Research) Received from Various Sources by
Liberal Arts Colleges, 1959–60

Source and Purpose of Income	Percent of Net Income	
	Publicly Controlled Institutions	Privately Controlled Institutions
Student tuition and fees...........	17.7	65.0
Federal Government:		
Veterans' tuition and fees.......	.1	.1
Land-grant institutions..........	.3	.0
Research.......................	.0	.0
Other purposes.................	.6	.6
State governments................	70.9	.5
Local governments................	7.6	.2
Endowment earnings..............	.2	10.1
Private gifts and grants...........	.7	19.7
Subtotal........................	**97.9**	**96.2**
Related activities..................	1.1	1.4
Sales and services.................	.4	.2
Other educational and general....	.6	2.1
Total educational and general...	**100.0**	**100.0**

Source: From Table 8 "Analysis of income for educational and general purposes (except research) by source, and by control and type of institution: Aggregate United States, 1959–60," U.S. Office of Education, *Financial Statistics of Institutions of Higher Education, 1959-60, Receipts, Expenditures, and Property*, pp. 21–22.

from state and local governments, and 17.7 percent from student tuition and fees. Private liberal arts colleges derived 65 percent from student tuition and fees, 10.1 percent from endowment earnings, and 19.7 percent from private gifts and grants. The current trend is to increase tuition and fees in both public and private colleges and universities, but the degree to which the public college should rely on tuition and fees as a major source of income is controversial. It is argued by some leading authorities that it is in the public interest to keep tuition and fees low in publicly supported institutions, thereby extending the opportunities for post-high school education as widely as possible. Others argue that the individual is a primary beneficiary of higher education and should bear the major part of the cost of his education. The weight of the argument is in favor of keeping tuition and fees low in public higher institutions. If, however, tuition and fees in public colleges continue to rise, a corresponding increase in student aid must be provided, or promising students of limited means will be deprived of opportunities for advanced education, and society will be the loser.

Past experience reflected in these data suggests that a new *publicly* supported senior college might expect to derive about 18 percent of its income for educational and general expense from student tuition and fees, about 72 percent from state and local governments and the balance in small amounts from miscellaneous sources. Typically, a *private* college derives approximately two-thirds of its income for educational and general purposes from student tuition fees, about 20 percent from private gifts and grants, and about 10 percent from endowment earnings. The remainder will come from other sources. However, in the initial stages of its operation, a new college will not have its full complement of students, nor is it likely to have a substantial endowment fund, therefore, it will need to increase the proportions of income derived from other sources.

Since private gifts and grants play an important role, particularly in financing a private college, this source needs to be examined further. A report of the Council for Financial Aid to Education, Inc. presents recent and comprehensive data on voluntary support of higher education.[7] According to this report, 1,064 colleges and universities of all sizes and types received $1,244,815,734 in voluntary contributions in 1964-65.

Looking specifically at private liberal arts colleges, the per-

---

[7] *1964-65 Voluntary Support of American Colleges and Universities* (New York: Council for Financial Aid to Education, Inc., 1966).

centage of funds derived from each of several sources by private coeducational colleges, private women's colleges, and private men's colleges is as follows:

Source	365 Private Coed Colleges	140 Private Women's Colleges	67 Private Men's Colleges
Alumni or Alumnae . .	16.9%	34.3%	29.8%
General Welfare Foundations	20.9	24.3	22.3
Non-Alumni Individuals	31.7	23.6	22.2
Business Corporations	12.4	8.1	15.3
Religious Denominations . . .	13.8	7.6	3.8
Non-Alumni, Non-Church Groups .	2.5	1.5	1.2
Other Sources	1.8	0.6	5.4

For all types of institutions, the report indicates that approximately one-third of the funds were unrestricted as to purpose, 26.8 percent were designated for physical plant, 11.2 percent for research, 16.7 percent for student financial aid and faculty staff compensation, and 12.5 percent for other purposes. For private colleges the allocation between the current operation and capital funds was as follows:

Type of College	Current Operation	Capital Funds
Private Coed Colleges	35.8%	64.2%
Private Women's Colleges . .	37.6	62.4
Private Men's Colleges	18.9	81.1

In summary:

1. A new public senior college will derive its financial support chiefly from state and local governments, and secondarily from student tuition and fees. As has been noted, it is in the interest of the public welfare to keep tuition and fees low.

2. A new private senior college will look to student tuition and fees and to private philanthropy for its main support. Initially it probably will not have a large endowment nor will it have an alumni body such as those from which established private colleges get substantial support.

79

ESTIMATING CAPITAL CONSTRUCTION COSTS

There should be assurance of ample funds for physical facilities as well as operating costs before final steps are taken to establish a college. Impressive instances could be cited of new colleges that have had to limp along because of short-sighted financial planning.

Several methods of estimating the outlay per student for physical facilities may enable those concerned with planning a new college to determine within a broad range the magnitude of financing involved.

The most recent report of the U. S. Office of Education College and University Facilities Survey contains data on the cost of new construction and rehabilitation projects completed or planned by new higher institutions during the period 1961-65.[8] Using the full-time equivalent enrollment for 1965-66, the cost per full-time student for new four-year liberal arts colleges was $4,287.

The *Master Plan for Higher Education in California, 1960-75,* reports the net capital outlay costs per student for a state college enrolling 5,000 students to be $4,280; for a state college enrolling 10,000 students, $4,050; and for a state college enrolling 20,000 full-time students, $3,750.[9]

There are more precise ways of estimating such costs. One of these is to estimate the number of square feet of space per student required for various functions and the cost of construction per square foot. In applying this to individual institutions, of course, consideration must be given to the fact that the number of square feet per student will be affected by the characteristics of the institution's program, methods of instruction, and the out-of-class space needs of students and faculty. For example, one program may be more heavily weighted with laboratory sciences than another; one may stress large lecture groups while another places major emphasis on independent study and seminars; one may have a large percentage of commuting students while another has a student body that is largely residential. Costs of construction also will vary by geographical regions. These factors create institutional variations, but they can be defined with considerable accuracy, if a careful analysis is made of the proposed college's program and site.

---

[8]Leslie F. Robbins and W. Robert Bokelman, *Enrollment and Facilities of New Colleges and Universities Opening Between 1961 and 1965, College and University Facilities Survey: Part 5,* U.S. Office of Education Circular No. 773 (Washington, D. C.: U.S. Government Printing Office, 1965).

[9]*A Master Plan for Higher Education in California, 1960-75* (Sacramento, California: State Department of Education, 1960).

Table 6—Standard Floor Areas Per Full-time Student Proposed by the California Restudy for State Colleges in California

Type of Building Space	Net Square Feet Per Full-time Student—Campus-wide Average									
	For 2,000 Students	For 3,000 Students	For 4,000 Students	For 5,000 Students	For 6,000 Students	For 8,000 Students	For 10,000 Students	For 15,000 Students	For 20,000 Students	For 25,000 Students
Classrooms, including seminars[a]	11.0	10.4	10.0	9.6	9.6	9.6	9.6	9.6	9.6	9.6
Teaching labs, including service[a]	22.9	21.0	19.3	17.6	17.6	17.6	17.6	17.6	17.6	17.6
Subtotal	**33.9**	**31.4**	**29.3**	**27.2**	**27.2**	**27.2**	**27.2**	**27.2**	**27.2**	**27.2**
Library and study hall[b]	10.5	10.5	10.5	10.5	10.3	10.1	9.9	9.7	9.5	9.4
Physical education[b]	12.0	11.0	10.5	10.2	9.7	9.0	8.6	7.4	6.6	6.0
Military sciences[b]	2.0	2.0	2.0	2.0	2.0	1.9	1.9	1.8	1.7	1.6
Offices—institutional departments[a]	10.4	9.9	9.4	9.0	9.0	9.0	9.0	9.0	9.0	9.0
Cumulative subtotal	**68.8**	**64.8**	**61.7**	**58.9**	**58.2**	**57.2**	**56.6**	**55.1**	**54.0**	**53.2**
Offices—general administration	5.0	4.4	4.0	3.8	3.6	3.4	3.2	2.8	2.5	2.3
Cafeteria and student center[b]	8.0	8.0	8.0	8.0	7.8	7.6	7.5	7.0	6.5	6.2
Health service[b]	1.0	1.0	1.0	0.9	0.9	0.9	0.9	0.8	0.8	0.7
Auditorium and theater[c]	2.0	2.0	2.0	2.0	2.0	1.8	1.4	0.9	0.7	0.6
Cumulative subtotal	**84.8**	**80.2**	**76.7**	**73.6**	**72.5**	**70.9**	**69.6**	**66.6**	**64.5**	**63.0**
Shops, storage, misc.	5.1	4.8	4.6	4.4	4.4	4.3	4.2	4.0	3.9	3.8
Total	**89.9**	**85.0**	**81.3**	**78.0**	**76.9**	**75.2**	**73.8**	**70.6**	**68.4**	**66.8**

[a] Excluding physical education and military sciences.
[b] Including offices and all other directly related space (including classrooms for physical education and military sciences).
[c] Excluding areas classified as general classrooms or as teaching laboratories for drama and music.

Source: Adapted from Table 36, "Standard Floor Areas Per Full-time Student in State Colleges and the University of California, According to Size," *A Restudy of the Needs of California in Higher Education,* 1955, p. 352.

81

The standard floor areas which were proposed for California colleges in the restudy of the needs of California higher education are summarized in Table 6. For a college of 2,000 students the recommendations were 11.0 square feet per student for classrooms and 22.9 square feet per student for teaching laboratories. These guidelines are considered unusually restrictive and probably should be looked upon as representing a minimal figure. It is noted that the proposed standards vary according to institutional size.

Jamrich studied 53 liberal arts colleges in the North Central area of the United States and found the actual space for general use in those institutions averaged 19.1 square feet for general classrooms and 9.5 square feet for instructional laboratories per full-time student enrolled.[10] These figures are quite different from those proposed in the California *Restudy*. It should also be noted that the figures reflect what actually exists at the colleges surveyed, rather than what the colleges might consider desirable.

After deciding upon the square feet per student which best "fits" the program at the proposed new college, the next step in arriving at an estimate of cost per student of new facilities is to multiply the number of square feet per student by the construction cost per square foot. Two variables that affect this computation are differences in construction costs in different geographic areas and differences in costs according to the function the space is designed to serve.

Table 7 summarizes estimated costs of new construction per square foot by size of institution and by geographic area. These data clearly indicate that the region in which a new senior college is to be located is an important consideration in projecting the cost of physical facilities. Costs were lower in the Southeast than in any other region for institutions of all sizes.

Table 8 presents the cost per square foot of new construction for types of colleges and universities, broken down by public and private, by geographic region of the nation, and by type of space constructed. These data, like those in the preceding table, indicate that, in general, construction costs were highest in the North Atlantic area and lowest in the Southeast region. Since these data include all types of institutions, it is not possible to derive a precise figure for senior liberal arts colleges. It may be reasonable to assume, however, that if one disregards the cost listed for "research" space, the space costs shown will not differ greatly from those for new senior liberal arts colleges.

---

[10]John X. Jamrich, *To Build or Not to Build: A Report on the Utilization and Planning of Instructional Facilities in Small Colleges* (New York: Educational Facilities Laboratory, n.d.), p. 27.

Table 7—Estimated Cost Per Square Foot of New Construction Projects, 1960–61 to 1965–66

Region	Institutional Enrollment					
	Below 500	500–999	1,000–2,499	2,500–4,999	5,000–9,999	10,000 and over	Average
North Atlantic..........	$20.50	$20.90	$22.50	$23.10	$26.90	$28.00	$24.80
Great Lakes and Plains..........	17.30	19.50	19.00	18.90	23.40	25.70	22.40
Southeast..........	13.00	16.90	16.10	17.80	19.00	20.50	17.70
West and Southwest..........	22.80	17.80	23.60	20.00	22.30	24.60	22.50
Outlying Parts..........	40.80					19.70	26.40
National Average..........							**22.10**

Source: U.S. Office of Education, *College and University Facilities Survey, Part 4* (Washington: Government Printing Office, 1964), p. 87.

83

Table 8—Cost per Square Foot for New Construction Planned for 1961–65 by Higher Education Institutions, by Control, Region, and Functional Group of Facilities

Region	Instructional	Research	General	Residential	Other Auxiliary	All Types Combined
PUBLIC INSTITUTIONS						
North Atlantic	$23.80	$28.80	$22.80	$18.70	$24.00	$22.50
Great Lakes and Plains	24.00	33.00	23.50	18.40	22.30	22.30
Southeast	18.00	23.10	17.50	15.10	18.00	17.10
West and Southwest	23.90	33.70	19.60	18.40	23.80	22.90
Outlying Parts	25.30	.....	.....	(*)	.....	(*)
National Average	**22.70**	**31.40**	**20.60**	**17.50**	**21.80**	**21.40**
PRIVATE INSTITUTIONS						
North Atlantic	27.80	38.30	19.50	22.40	22.50	25.80
Great Lakes and Plains	23.80	34.80	26.80	18.80	21.30	22.60
Southeast	21.40	30.30	15.80	16.00	16.50	19.20
West and Southwest	23.30	31.00	13.40	19.10	22.20	21.00
Outlying Parts	.....	.....	.....	.....	.....	.....
National Average	**25.10**	**35.40**	**18.70**	**19.80**	**21.20**	**23.20**
ALL INSTITUTIONS COMBINED						
North Atlantic	26.50	35.90	20.30	21.30	23.00	24.80
Great Lakes and Plains	23.90	33.70	24.60	18.50	21.80	22.40
Southeast	19.10	25.00	16.80	15.30	17.50	17.70
West and Southwest	23.70	33.20	17.80	18.60	23.40	22.50
Outlying Parts	25.30	.....	.....	(*)	.....	(*)
National Average	**23.60**	**33.00**	**19.80**	**18.50**	**21.50**	**22.10**

*Insufficient data.

Source: Adapted from Table CC "Cost per square foot for new construction planned for 1961–65 by higher education institutions, by control, region, and functional group of facilities," U.S. Office of Education, *College and University Facilities Survey, Part 4,* p. 90.

Another important factor in planning for capital construction is inflation. Cost norms must be adjusted upward to take account of cost increases between the years upon which the norms were based and the year in which construction contracts will be let. Table 9 shows the changes in average cost per square foot which occurred between 1958-59 and 1961-65.

Table 9—Actual and projected cost per square foot for new construction at higher education institutions, selected facilities

Primary Function	Actual 1958-59	Projected 1961-65
All Functions.................................	$19.00	$22.10
Instructional..	20.30	23.60
Classroom buildings...........................	20.00	23.10
Library..	17.70	23.00
Instructional laboratories......................	23.00	25.70
Research..	24.00	33.00
General...	22.70	19.80
Residential......................................	16.70	18.50
Married students' apartments..................	13.70	15.60
Men's residence halls..........................	17.80	18.60
Women's residence halls.......................	16.80	18.90
Other auxiliary facilities.........................	19.80	21.50
College unions..................................	18.90	22.60
Food service facilities..........................	23.00	22.10

Source: Adapted from Table EE, "Actual and projected cost per square foot for new construction at higher education institutions: selected facilities," U.S. Office of Education, *College and University Facilities Survey, Part 4,* p. 91.

It is apparent, then, that a rough estimate of cost can be made by using square feet of space per student to determine total space needs and then applying the square foot cost of construction appropriate to the region in order to estimate total cost. Shown below are two estimates of costs for a college of 1,000 students, one based upon the more generous estimate of 125 square feet per student used by the U. S. Office of Education in projecting space needs to 1970 and the other based upon the more conservative figure of 89.9 square feet per student derived from the California *Restudy.*

Regions	125 square feet per student	89.9 square feet per student
North Atlantic	$2,812,500	$2,022,750
Great Lakes and Plains . . .	2,375,000	1,708,100
Southeast	2,012,500	1,447,390
West and Southwest	2,950,000	2,121,640

This procedure can be refined in several ways. The space requirements for different functions — instruction, research, general, residential, and auxiliary — may be computed separately. The cost per square foot of construction for each function also can be computed by geographic regions.

A Colorado manual suggests an annual 2.7 percent rate of increase for changes in building costs — labor, materials, etc.[11] This factor will vary by time periods and regions and will have to be determined for each instance.

It must also be borne in mind that the costs for site acquisition and development, architectural and engineering fees, and movable equipment usually must be added to the costs discussed thus far. The Colorado manual contains a suggestion that the increments for these items as a percent of construction costs be: site development, 5 percent; architectural and engineering fees, 6 percent; and movable equipment, 10 to 20 percent. These items together increase the total estimated cost by 21 to 31 percent.

The cost of library books warrants special comment. Library construction costs do not differ materially from the costs of other physical facilities, and the preceding discussion of capital expenditures for physical facilities included library buildings.

The initial cost of books is quite another matter, and the outlay for books required for a library ready for use when a new college opens is of such a magnitude that it must be taken into account in estimating capital expenditures.

A rough estimate of the size of a new college library may be derived from analyses that have been made of library holdings. On this point Lyle [12] notes than an analysis of the statistics on small college libraries indicates that 50,000 well chosen volumes are required to give effective support to the instructional program. This is an estimate for an enrollment of 600 students. For every additional 200 students he suggests that 10,000 volumes be added. Most new colleges cannot expect to have this total number of volumes when they open. Building a library is a long-term procedure. The content of the library must be determined by the demands of the educational program and by the anticipated size of the enrollment. If the enrollment is to be built up sequentially

[11]Association of State Institutions of Higher Education in Colorado, *Manual of Procedures and Standards for Building Space and Capital Outlay Planning in Colorado* (Boulder, Colorado: The Association, 1963). *Note:* The Association has been superseded by the Colorado Commission on Higher Education, with headquarters in Denver.

[12]Guy R. Lyle, *The President, the Professor and the College Library* (New York: The H. W. Wilson Company, 1959).

from the freshman to the senior year, the initial library requirements will be less than if students are enrolled at all levels from the beginning. A librarian will have a full-time job building a library of 25,000 or 30,000 well selected volumes over a period of several years prior to the opening of a new college. Even this number, however, represents a sizable capital expenditure.

A rule of thumb for estimating costs is that the average cost of a library book is approximately $6.00 and an additional $6.00 is required to put each volume on the shelf ready for use. At a rate of $12.00 per volume, 30,000 volumes would require an expenditure of $360,000. The introduction of automated procedures may save staff time, but there is no indication that costs will be reduced.

No attempt is made to provide precise formulae for determining construction costs for new facilities. The discussion may be of value, however, in providing broad guidelines for estimating cost and in suggesting a number of the specific factors that must be taken into account in such estimates.

Based upon the foregoing discussion, it is possible to hypothesize a rough estimate of the capital costs of a four-year college intended to serve an enrollment of 1,000 students in the Southeast:

Basic construction (125 square feet per student)	$2,012,500	
Adjustment for inflation (2.7% annually for 5 years) . . .	271,688	
Current basic construction costs . . .		$2,284,188
Add for land, site development, equipment, architect, etc. (26%) .		593,889
Library books (30,000 at $12.00) . .		360.000
Total		$3,238,077

SOURCES OF FUNDS FOR CAPITAL CONSTRUCTION

Sources of capital construction funds differ significantly from sources of operating funds. Table 10 shows the sources of funds in percentages for planned construction at colleges and universities of all types during the period 1960-65.

Public institutions estimated that 59 percent of their capital construction funds would come from state and Federal appropriations; private institutions estimated that 54 percent of their capital construction funds would come from gifts and grants. Borrowing was a major secondary source for both public and private institutions, and government appropriations (especially from Federal sources) also were an important secondary source for private institutions.

Table 10—Sources, in percentages, of estimated funds for instructional, research and general facilities combined, by control: Aggregate U.S., fall 1960 to fall 1965.

	Public	Private
Total..	100.0%	100.0%
Government appropriations and tax levies........	59.2	11.0
State and local.................................	(56.0)	(2.6)
Federal...	(3.2)	(8.4)
Borrowing...	18.6	10.7
General obligation bonds.......................	(17.7)	(5.3)
From commercial lenders.......................	(0.4)	(3.0)
From endowment and other campus funds......	(0.5)	(2.4)
Gifts and grants..................................	3.5	54.4
All other known sources..........................	4.2	4.3
Sources not yet known...........................	14.5	19.6

Source: U.S. Office of Education. *College and University Physical Facilities Series* July 1962, Table 2.

This chapter has outlined major factors to be considered in estimating the magnitude of financing required in planning new colleges. Illustrative data have been presented, first on operating costs, with a discussion of sources of support for these expenditures. Secondly, suggestions have been offered for estimating construction costs, along with data on the sources of capital outlay funds.

For a new college enrolling 1,000 students, the data suggest an annual operating budget of at least one to one and a half million dollars. Capital construction for such an institution, it is shown, may be expected to involve expenditures in the neighborhood of three and a quarter million dollars.

CHAPTER 4

PITFALLS IN PLANNING A NEW COLLEGE

The preceding discussion is designed to provide information that will be helpful to individuals, state agencies, community committees, church boards, or others who may either contemplate or be committed to the establishment of a new senior college. The point of view governing the discussion is that sound planning is a pre-requisite to the development of a college of distinction. At various points danger signals have been raised. Some potential dangers are of such magnitude that they may appropriately be characterized as "pitfalls." For the sake of emphasis they are summarized here.

Among pitfalls that should be scrupulously avoided are the following:

1. Proceeding without adequate justification. This danger has special relevance to the private college either independent or church related. Ambitious individuals get the idea that a college would be a valuable asset to their community. They promote the idea by enlisting community sentiment and by getting the endorsement of leading citizens. No analytical studies are made to determine the need for or the feasibility of establishing the proposed college. As a consequence, more independent colleges than is generally realized are conceived and born in the wrong places for the wrong reasons.

   The same criticism, though to a lesser degree, must be made of church leaders in church districts, conferences or states who proceed to promote the establishment of a new church-related college without determining the need for the institution in relation to the colleges already operating under the denomination's auspices and without relation to criteria by which to justify their decision.

New state colleges, generally, are established in response to needs demonstrated by state and/or area studies. Such studies are made by state boards of regents, by state commissions created by the legislature or by citizens' organizations that have an interest in promoting the welfare of the state. But here again, there are states in which powerful politicians have persuaded the legislature to authorize and support the establishment of a college as a political favor without adequate justification. This is pure folly in the guise of community benefit.

2. Another pitfall is to proceed with the establishment of a new college without a clear perception of the kind of college that is envisaged. This limitation is most often reflected in the lack of clearly stated purposes or in a statement that is too visionary to serve as a guide in the development of the institution. Purposes should be formulated not for propaganda use but as the guiding philosophy and undergirding principles of the institution.

3. There appears to be a widespread misconception that the name university gives an institution some kind of superior status. There has been a strong trend in recent years for state colleges to aspire to and gain university status, in too many instances, before they have developed an essential basic liberal arts program. There are also a number of so-called private universities that are in fact liberal arts colleges. In a few instances these institutions have changed their names from "university" to "college" to conform to their function. A new senior college should have its function and program so clearly defined that there will be no question about its place in the scheme of higher education. To create unjustifiable aspirations by using the designation "university" for a new institution that is in fact to be a senior college is a pitfall of major consequences.

4. The mistake is sometimes made of using a college of distinction as a model. One frequently hears the comment that this new college is designed to be the Harvard of the Midwest, the Yale of the South, or another

Oberlin or Antioch. Certainly, in planning a new college the characteristics of higher institutions of distinction and how they have achieved distinction should be given full consideration. The experiences of these institutions may provide profitable guidelines. It should not be assumed, however, that the Harvard or University of Chicago plan of general education can be transplanted to a new campus. Each new college must have its own design, a design that is indigenous to the purposes of the college in its locale; a design that may, nevertheless, incorporate elements from the best colleges in the nation provided they are appropriate to the purposes and plans of the new institution.

5. Even more hazardous to the fate of a new college is lack of imagination, of innovation, in planning. Here again the key factor may be the tendency to imitate a conventional, conservative college. The social scene is changing at such a rate that the new college that is imitatively conventional will be out of date before it ever gets under way. In fact higher educational institutions generally are so conservative that they have failed to keep pace with changing social needs. A new college should be in the vanguard of the academic procession rather than merely trailing along.

6. It is a mistake to draft plans for a new college without involving in the early stages those who will be responsible for its operation. Key administrative personnel should have an important part in designing the general administrative structure and, with the aid of a few well chosen faculty members, the designing of the overall plan of the educational program. As has been emphasized repeatedly, the educational philosophy and the educational functions of the college should govern the design of educational facilities. To invite a president, academic dean, and business officer to take over after the pattern is set is often to invite a restructuring of the pattern.

7. It should not be assumed that a plan once made is fixed and final. The data and premises on which the plan is based must be continuously reviewed. Changes in the constituency or changes due to economic and resource developments of an area may suggest modifications of

an educational program. New technological developments may have important implications for methods of teaching as may new understandings of the learner or of the learning process. A common oversight in planning a new college is the omission of any provision for continuing study of emerging needs and for a continuing evaluation of achievements in relation to purposes.

8. A serious limitation that exists in many colleges and universities throughout the nation is the lack of communication. This is manifested in various ways: inadequate communication between the central administration and the trustees, the faculty and the students; and such a high degree of compartmentalization of the program that faculty members live and work in comparative isolation. Though more attention is being given to public relations there is still inadequate communication between institutions and alumni, constituents and other groups on whom they are dependent and whose interests they serve. The communication between a college and its public is not a matter of extravagant advertising but of providing basic information about all phases of its program and operation. There is no better way, in fact, no other way, of developing and holding public confidence and support.

9. The intrusion of the heavy hand of special interests is inimical to the best interests of a new college. This heavy hand may be exercised in the selection of the location or site of the college, in the determination of the kind of college, and even in the administration of the college. It may be the hand of a legislator, of a powerful industrialist or financier, or of a bishop or evangelist. The first step in offsetting these intrusions by special interests is to establish criteria that will govern every step in the establishment of the new college.

10. Flexibility in physical facilities is the counterpart of flexibility in the educational program. The pitfall here is that (a) architects may be employed who are inexperienced in designing educational plants; (b) that building authorities not oriented to educational institutions impose inappropriate building standards; (c) that architects who are experienced in designing college plants are not included in early planning confer-

ences and therefore are not fully oriented to the purposes, program and general spirit of the new college.

11. Avant-garde architecture may have a novelty appeal, but the real test is how well it serves the purposes and program of the college. The limitations of conventional college buildings have been well documented but these limitations arise more from construction and space arrangement than from the style of the buildings. The conventional style need not be abandoned because of space and structural limitations if by appropriate adaptations it can serve well educational needs. New designs should be explored for their inherent values but to adopt extreme designs either as a credit to an architect or as a declaration of departure from the conventional may be a dubious procedure.

12. Faith is an indispensable element in conceiving and planning a new college. There is a pitfall, however, of relying on the "substance of things hoped for and the evidence of things not seen" to such a degree that plans without "substance" may develop. In other words, the assurance of adequate and sound financing is a *sine qua non* in planning a new college. A college is not a missionary enterprise and cannot operate on a missionary budget.

The need for new colleges becomes more and more apparent. To serve this need new colleges must be good colleges. They must be good not in terms of the excellence ascribed to great universities but good in the sense that they have clearly defined missions, programs appropriate to their mission, faculties, facilities and resources that will enable them to maintain a position of leadership in their respective fields of endeavor in a society in which change calls for direction.

ANNOTATED BIBLIOGRAPHY

State-Wide Planning and Coordination:

Brumbaugh, A. J. *State-Wide Planning and Coordination of Higher Education.* Atlanta, Georgia: Southern Regional Education Board, 1963.

A description and analysis of the types and functions of agencies for state-wide planning and coordination of public colleges and universities; an evaluation of the several plans; a summary of requirements for effective state-wide planning and coordination and a summary of salaries paid the chief administrative officers and staff members of coordinating agencies in nine Southern states.

Brumbaugh, A. J., and Blee, Myron R. *Higher Education and Florida's Future,* Vol. I: *Recommendations and General Staff Report.* Gainesville, Florida: University of Florida Press, 1956.

Summarizes the major findings and recommendations of a comprehensive state-wide study of higher education in Florida. This study provided the basis for the development of a network of community junior colleges and for the establishment of several new universities. It also led to further studies designed to define the role and scope of each publicly supported university.

California State Department of Education. *A Restudy of the Needs of California in Higher Education.* Sacramento, California: California State Department of Education, 1955.

A comprehensive study covering needs for higher education measured by population trends; the functions and programs of higher education in California; the government administration and coordination of public higher education in the state; physical facilities and future plant needs; the ability of the state to support higher education and an analysis of expenses for educational and general purposes. This provided the basis for the development of a coordinated system of higher education in California. It also served as an important reference and model for other state-wide studies.

California State Department of Education. *A Study of the Need for Additional Centers of Public Higher Education in California.* Sacramento, California: California State Department of Education, 1957.

This represents an intermediate stage between the *Restudy of Needs of California in Higher Education* and the adoption of a *Master Plan for Higher Education in California.* It is a valuable source of procedures and criteria in determining the need for junior colleges, state colleges, and additional university campuses.

California State Department of Education. *A Master Plan for Higher Education in California.* Sacramento, California: California State Department of Education, 1960.

This master plan is a sequel to earlier studies of higher education needs in California. It deals with the structure, functions, and coordination of higher education in California and considers in some detail specific issues involved in providing a system of higher education adequate to the needs of the state. A good example of comprehensive state-wide planning.

Pennsylvania State Board of Education. *Elements of a Master Plan for Higher Education in Pennsylvania*. Harrisburg, Pennsylvania: Pennsylvania State Board of Education, 1965.

A report of a panel of consultants appointed "to study higher education in Pennsylvania and to make recommendations on what might be included in the Commonwealth's Master Plan for Higher Education." The study contains less statistical data than do most state-wide studies. It does present sound principles of planning that have relevance to planning in other states.

State of California. *Projections of Enrollment for California Institutions of Higher Education: 1960-1975*. Sacramento, California: State of California, Department of Finance, 1960.

The title indicates the content of this report. It provides a body of data essential to state-wide planning.

State of Illinois. *Reports of Master Plan Committees*. Springfield, Illinois: State of Illinois Board of Higher Education, 1963.

A series of Master Plan Committee reports to the Illinois Board of Higher Education. Each report covers a partial phase of master planning — enrollments, admission and retention of students, faculty, programs, research, two-year colleges, extension and public service, vocational and technical education, physical facilities and finance. A rich resource of information and ideas related to the development of a state-wide master plan.

U. S. Office of Education. *Higher Education in Connecticut*, Vols. I and II: *Report of a Survey*. Washington, D. C.: U. S. Office of Education, 1964.

A report of a state-wide study of higher education. Volume I contains working papers and extensive data from which conclusions and recommendations are drawn. Volume II presents in brief some of the major findings and the complete set of recommendations. An especially important reference because of the comprehensive body of recommendations.

The University of the State of New York. *The Regents Statewide Plan for the Expansion and Development of Higher Education: 1964*. Albany, New York: The University of the State of New York, The State Education Department, 1965.

Another of an increasing number of state-wide plans to enable the state to provide for future higher educational needs of individuals and for the state's social and economic needs. The role of various types of higher institutions is identified, plans of individual institutions are renewed and estimates of costs are made and proposals to meet the needs of the state are made.

Wilson, Logan. *Emerging Patterns in Higher Education.* Washington, D. C.: American Council on Education, 1965.

A comprehensive treatment by a number of recognized authorities of (1) emerging patterns of institutional administration and accompanying charges in attitudes; (2) emerging patterns of state-wide organization of public higher education; (3) inter-state and inter-institutional agreements; (4) approaches to the improvement of higher education at the national level and some problems that arise.

Campus Planning — Purposes and Programs:

Coordinating Council for Higher Education. *A Comparison of the Trimester and Quarter Calendars for Year Round Operation of Public Higher Education in California.* Sacramento and San Francisco, California: Coordinating Council for Higher Education, 1964.

A study of the benefits and problems of year-round operation of higher institutions; a comparison of the trimester and quarter calendars in terms of education service, flexibility, distribution of enrollments, educational programs, administration, articulation and costs. A number of other studies relating to year-round operation are noted in the appendix.

Current Issues in Higher Education, 1962, 1963, 1964, 1965. G. Kerry Smith, (ed.) Washington, D. C.: Association for Higher Education, National Education Association.

The Proceedings of the annual National Conferences on Higher Education by the Association for Higher Education for the years indicated. The papers and summaries of discussions of many aspects of higher education have implications for planning new colleges. Several that are especially relevant are cited in this brochure.

Dressel, Paul L. *The Undergraduate Curriculum in Higher Education.* New York: Center for Applied Research in Education, Inc., 1963.

An examination of issues relating to the college curriculum. The author deals with current curricula in undergraduate colleges, the conflict between "vocational" and "liberal" emphases; and with suggestions for curriculum study and development. An important reference for those engaged in curriculum planning or revision.

Mayhew, Lewis B. *The Smaller Liberal Arts College.* New York: The Center for Applied Research in Education, Inc., 1962.

A realistic appraisal of the status and role of the small liberal arts college in a period of rapid social change. Some of the major issues presented relate to the faculty—characteristics and conditions of service; the curriculum—distortions and suggested remedies; student personnel services; the functions and relationships of administrative personnel; finances. A good source of ideas for any one interested in improving a small private liberal arts college or in establishing a new one.

McGrath, Earl J., and Russell, Charles H. *Are Liberal Arts Colleges Becoming Professional Schools.* New York: Bureau of Publications, Teachers College, Columbia University, 1958.

An analysis of the broadening of the classical liberal arts curriculum to incorporate professional subjects. The authors do not decry this development but rather conclude that "the consanguinity of liberal and professional studies in a college community is a priceless desideration." They do, however, point out certain risks in present developments. They also emphasize the need for continuing education after graduation from college.

McGrath, Earl J. *Memo to a College Faculty Member.* New York: Bureau of Publications, Teachers College, Columbia University, 1961.

One of a series of studies published by the Institute of Higher Education of Teachers College, Columbia University. This one presents the findings in a study of the curricular offerings and costs of instruction in fourteen independent liberal arts colleges. Of special significance for program planning in a new senior college.

McGrath, Earl J. *The Liberal Arts College's Responsibility for the Individual Student.* New York: Teachers Colleges Press, 1966.

A conference report focused on needed changes in policy and practice to provide educational experiences appropriate for the present generation of students. The report includes papers by distinguished educators on a variety of topics such as emotional stability of students, testing and counseling students, development of social responsibility and new concepts of institutional goals for students.

McGrath, Earl J. (ed.) *Cooperative Long-Range Planning in Liberal Arts Colleges.* New York: Bureau of Publications, Teachers College, Columbia University, 1964.

A report of a conference in which representatives of liberal arts colleges, mostly presidents, examined with the guidance of consultants a number of aspects of the liberal arts college. The report presents the papers on quality and cost, a continuing program of institutional research, tuition, admissions policies, involving faculty members in formulating institutional policies, economy and change as factors in institutional development, and the pursuit of excellence.

Ruml, Beardsley, and Morrison, Donald H. *Memo to a College Trustee.* New York: McGraw-Hill Book Company, Inc., 1959.

A report by two recognized authorities of observations and criticisms of past policies and practices in liberal arts colleges. The authors consider the role of trustees, the functions of the college, and they make suggestions for improvements in curriculum and instruction to perform this function more effectively. They propose models of curricula that they believe will enable a college to attract an excellent faculty and to pay salaries commensurate with faculty competence.

Sanford, Nevitt (ed.) *The American College.* New York: John Wiley and Sons, Inc., 1962.

This volume is characterized as a psychological and social interpretation of the higher learning. A large number of recognized authorities participated in producing this comprehensive analysis and appraisal of a number of aspects of higher education. The scope of the volume may be gathered from a notation of some of the major areas covered, e.g. The Entering Student; Academic Procedures; Student Society and Student Culture; Student Performance in Relation to Educational Objectives; Interactions of Students and Educators; The Effects of College Education; Higher Education and the Social Context. As is suggested by these broad areas, this is an important source of information for persons concerned with plans for a new college.

Sloman, Albert E. *A University in the Making*. New York: Oxford University Press, 1964.

An account of the philosophy underlying a new university in England and plans for its development. A good example of the kind of analytical thinking that should, in fact must, provide the premises for a new higher institution.

Stickler, W. Hugh (ed.) *Experimental Colleges*. Tallahassee, Florida: Florida State University, 1964.

Report of a colloquium on experimental colleges in which were presented experimental plans in effect or contemplated in eleven different institutions. An excellent source of ideas for a new college that is interested in incorporating innovations into its educational program.

Wicke, Myron F. *The Church-Related College*. New York: The Center for Applied Research in Education, Inc., 1964.

A compact yet quite complete description and characterization of church-related colleges. Of particular value are profiles of selected colleges. Topics covered are purposes, programs, students and student services, finance, and control and organization. A final chapter on Prospect and Revision is especially significant for those who plan new private colleges.

Campus Planning — Physical Facilities:

Casebook on Campus Planning and Institutional Development: Ten Institutions: How They Did It. Compiled by John B. Rork and Leslie F. Robbins. U. S. Office of Education Circular No. 667. Washington, D. C.: U. S. Government Printing Office, 1962.

Presents ten case studies of procedures employed and problems encountered in expanding an existing college or university, or in moving a college or university to a new site, or in planning and building a new higher institution. While the focus of the report is on physical facilities, the authors derive from the experiences of those institutions a number of principles that are relevant to planning a new institution.

College and University Facilities Survey. U. S. Office of Education. Washington, D. C.: U. S. Government Printing Office.

Part 1. *Cost and Financing of College and University Buildings,* 1959.

Part 2. *Planning for College and University Physical Plant Expansion 1956-70,* 1960.

Part 3. *Inventory of College and University Physical Facilities,* 1965.

Part 4. *College and University Enrollment and Facilities Survey 1961-65,* 1965.

Part 5. *Enrollment and Facilities of New Colleges and Universities Opening between 1961 and 1965,* 1965.

A comprehensive study of the aspects of higher education indicated by the titles of the several parts of the study. Parts 2 and 5, *Planning for College and University Physical Plant Expansion,* and *Enrollment and Facilities of New Colleges and Universities Opening between 1961 and 65,* contain extensive data that will be helpful in designing a new senior college. Among the relevant topics covered are projected enrollments, projected physical facilities, estimating costs of facilities, and equipment, the sources of capital and estimates of operating costs of a new institution.

Dober, Richard P. *Campus Planning.* New York: Reinhold Publishing Corporation, 1963.

A comprehensive and thorough presentation of (a) the factors involved in effective campus planning with excellent illustrations; (b) conditions that affect architectural design with illustrations from various campuses; (c) an inter-woven philosophical interpretation of principles that govern campus planning and architectural design. A valuable source book for anyone responsible for planning a new college.

Labor and Material Requirements for College Housing Construction. United States Department of Labor, Bureau of Labor Statistics. Washington, D. C.: U. S. Government Printing Office, 1965.

A study of the man hours required for fixed dollar volume ($1,000) of college housing construction. The report is based on findings in a survey of 43 college housing projects. The study also analyzed construction costs in terms of several structural types and combinations of materials.

Manual of Procedures and Standards for Building Space Planning and Capital Outlay Planning. Denver, Colorado: Colorado Commission on Higher Education, 1963.

A detailed guide to planning facilities for higher education in Colorado. The manual was developed by professional consultants in cooperation with the Association of State Institutions of Higher Education in Colorado. It contains many formulae for estimating space requirements for various educational functions and for estimating costs. It has a two-fold value in that it illustrates the type of planning that other states might well do and in that it provides data and formulae which with appropriate adaptations may be used elsewhere.

The manual is reported to be out of print but copies may be available through inter-library loan.

"Report of the Planning Commission for a New University at Boca Raton." Tallahassee, Florida: Board of Regents, 1961 (Mimeographed).

A plan for a university that articulates with junior colleges and offers no courses at the conventional freshman-sophomore level. A number of innovations are included such as the establishment of a learning resources center, provision for differential rates of student progress, inter-disciplinary programs, and the production and use of materials for television instruction.

Russell, John Dale, and Doi, James I. *Manual for Studies of Space Utilization in Colleges and Universities.* Ohio University, Athens, Ohio: American Association of Collegiate Registrars and Admissions Officers, 1959.

The title describes the purpose of this manual. It is widely used as an authoritative basis for studying space utilization.

College and University Administration:

American Council on Education. *College and University Business Administration*, Vol. I and II. Washington, D. C.: American Council on Education, 1952.

These two volumes prepared by national committees representative of various organizations of college and university business officers and related agencies under the aegis of the American Council on Education have been accepted as the authoritative guide to the business administration of higher educational institutions. Volume I is given to budgeting, accounting, and reporting on the financial operation of an institution. Volume II deals with specific business operations such as purchasing, plant insurance, auxiliary enterprises, student affairs, non-academic personnel, investment management, sponsored research and legal problems. Revised editions are due to appear in the near future.

Dodds, Harold W. *The Academic President: Educator or Caretaker.* New York: McGraw-Hill Book Company, Inc., 1962.

An analysis of the multiple responsibilities of the college or university president as an educational leader and effective administrator. The relationship of the president to the faculty on one hand and to the trustees on the other are considered in some detail. Only limited attention is given to the public relations aspect of his multiple functions. Very important suggestions are made relative to the selection of a new president.

Library Statistics of Colleges and Universities, 1963-64. U. S. Office of Education Circular No. 769, by Theodore Samore. Washington, D. C.: U. S. Government Printing Office, 1965.

Voluminous data classified by states and the names of institutions. Among the topics covered are holdings, expenditures, personnel, salaries, space. A valuable source of comparative data for purposes of planning or evaluating a college or university library.

Lyle, Gary R. *The Administration of the College Library.* New York: The H. W. Wilson Company, 1961.

A good source of information on the organization of a library, the various services that a library provides, personnel required, procedures in selecting books and periodicals, planning a library, building and equipment, and the evaluation of the college library.

Messersmith, James L. *Church-Related Boards Responsible for Higher Education.* U. S. Office of Education Bulletin No. 1964, No. 13. Washington, D. C.: U. S. Government Printing Office, 1964.

A comprehensive analysis of boards of higher education in non-public institutions. It treats types, size and functions of boards in general, and the plans for the organization and administration of higher education by particular religious denominations. An excellent source of information on current plans and practices in private institutions.

Mobberly, David G., and Wicke, Myron F. *The Deanship of the Liberal Arts College.* Nashville, Tennessee: Division of Higher Education, The Methodist Church, 1962.

A concise analysis of the relationships and responsibilities of the dean of a liberal arts college. Especially valuable in establishing a plan of administration in which the role of the dean must be defined.

Rauh, Morton A. *College and University Trusteeship.* Yellow Springs, Ohio: The Antioch Press, 1959.

Essentially a handbook for trustees designed to identify the major functions of trustees, the problems with which trustees deal, examples of practices followed by trustees in fulfilling their responsibilities.

Wicke, Myron F. *Handbook for Trustees.* Nashville, Tennessee: Division of Higher Education, Board of Education, The Methodist Church, 1962.

A succinct presentation of the areas of responsibility of boards of trustees and of guidelines for their effective operation.

Stickler, W. Hugh, and Carrothers, Milton W. *The Year-Round Calendar in Operation.* SREB Research Monograph No. 7. Atlanta, Georgia: Southern Regional Education Board, 1963.

A study of the status, trends, problems, and financial implications of the year-round calendar. The report presents case studies and conclusions based on analyses and observations made by the authors.

Woodburne, Lloyd S. *Principles of College and University Administration.* Stanford, California: Stanford University Press, 1958.

While this volume is focused on university organization and administration, it contains a number of principles and proposals that would be applicable to designing an administrative organization for a new college and for defining the functions of major administrative officers.

Financing Higher Education:

California State Department of Education. *California's Ability to Finance Higher Education 1960-1975.* Sacramento, California: California State Department of Education, 1961.

One of several studies growing out of the *Restudy of the Needs of Higher Education in California.* The report presents "projections of estimated revenues to the General Fund of the State of California . . .; projections of estimated expenditures for other claimants on the General Fund besides public higher education, on the basis of no change in the scope and quality of service rendered; and some measures of the relative fiscal effort of the several states in their support of public higher education." The substantive findings have special relevance to higher education in California but the methodology is applicable in other states.

Financial Statistics of Institutions of Higher Education 1959-60: Receipts, Expenditures, and Property. U. S. Office of Education Circular No. 744, by Felix H. I. Lindsay. Washington, D. C.: U. S. Government Printing Office, 1964.

A comprehensive body of financial data on (a) current fund income and expenditures in institutions of various sizes and types, (b) plant fund receipts and expenditures, (c) endowment and student loan funds. Since the data pertain to 1959-60, corrections need to be made for changes in the intervening years. The general pattern of income and expenditures has probably not changed materially.

"Is Higher Tuition the Answer?" *Financing Higher Education, Number 4.* Atlanta, Georgia: Southern Regional Education Board.

A presentation of arguments for and against expecting students to bear an increasing share of the cost of their college education by two leading authorities, Dr. John Dale Russell and Dr. Seymour Harris.

Miller, James L. *State Budgeting for Higher Education: The Use of Formulas and Cost Analysis.* Ann Arbor, Michigan: Institute of Public Administration, The University of Michigan, 1964.

An up-to-date authoritative monograph on the use of formulas and cost analyses in state budgeting for higher education. The major areas of the study are formulas in historical perspective, formulas in use in selected states, and the significance of formulas and cost analyses; a summary and evaluation of the procedure.

The Sixty College Study . . . . A Second Look. National Federation of College and University Business Officers Associations, 1960.

A comparative study of income and expenditures in sixty private colleges for the years 1953-1954 and 1957-1958. While the data are not strictly current they are important in that they give a comprehensive over-view of expenditures involved and sources of income in operating a private college.

Metz, Gustave Ernest. *Current Fund Expenditures.* Atlanta, Georgia: Southern Association of Colleges and Schools, 1964.

102

A summary and analysis of data on educational and general expenditures in 404 institutions that were members of the Southern Association of Colleges and Schools. The analyses provide normative data for use by the Commission Colleges of the Association. The data also have relevance for planning a new senior college in that they provide a basis for estimating operating costs of a new institution.

Salaries in Higher Education 1965-66. Washington, D. C.: Research Division, National Education Association, 1966.

The title suggests the content of this report. A valuable source of comparative data on faculty salaries.

Schietinger, E. F. *Fact Book on Higher Education in the South.* Atlanta, Georgia: Southern Regional Education Board, 1965.

A valuable source of data on a number of aspects of higher education in the Southern Region. The major topics on which extensive statistical information is presented are: population, institutions of higher education, enrollment, student finances; institutional finances, faculty, and graduate education. For purposes of comparison data for the nation are given. While the Fact Book is oriented to the Southern region it has applicability for planning.

Tickton, Sidney G. *A Ten-Year College Budget.* New York: Fund for the Advancement of Education, 1961.

An imaginative and practical approach to long-range budgeting. The author stresses factors that require long-range budgeting, the basic issues and concepts in long-range budgeting, accompanied by a specific case study and suggested forms.

1964-65 Voluntary Support of America's Colleges and Universities. New York: Council for Financial Aid to Education, 1966.

Reports amounts of voluntary support of America's colleges and universities. The amounts received by various types of institutions, the contributors, and purposes for which contributions were made. Of special value in estimating the amount and possible sources of voluntary support for a new senior college, public or private.